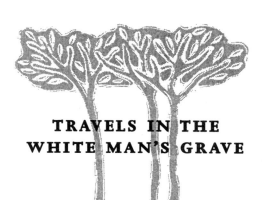

TRAVELS IN THE
WHITE MAN'S GRAVE

DONALD MacINTOSH

TRAVELS IN THE
WHITE MAN'S GRAVE

361882/966

Foreword by Richard Ingrams

NEIL WILSON PUBLISHING · GLASGOW · SCOTLAND

To the memory of
my father and grandfather
who nurtured my childhood curiosity
about those faraway places with
the strange-sounding names

First published by
Neil Wilson Publishing
303a The Pentagon Centre
36 Washington Street
GLASGOW
G3 8AZ
Tel: 0141-221-1117
Fax: 0141-221-5363
E-mail: nwp@cqm.co.uk
http://www.nwp.co.uk/

A catalogue record for this book is
available from the British Library.

ISBN 1-897784-83-X

The publisher acknowledges subsidy from the
Scottish Arts Council towards the publication of this volume.

Typeset in Monotype Joanna
Designed by Mark Blackadder
Chapter heading illustration by Sheila Cant
Printed by WSOY, Finland

CONTENTS

FOREWORD

This is the age of the professional and the specialist. In the world in which I live – magazine journalism and publishing – writing is considered an activity which is best left to the card-carrying members of the Union. The amateur, the outsider, the part-timer, is unlikely to get a look in.

One of my great pleasures, therefore, since helping to launch The Oldie in 1992, is the large amount of unsolicited material that has come my way – much of it from men and women who have taken up writing as a second career. And why not? Writing is something anyone can do – like photography. You need no special training, only a way with words, something that cannot be acquired at a university or evening class.

Few unsolicited submissions have given me so much pleasure as those of Donald MacIntosh. Not only was he a natural writer but he had a lifetime's experience in Africa to draw on. His stories of African life (some of which we published in The Oldie) were not only warm-hearted and witty. They conveyed the atmosphere of colonial Africa with a wealth of vivid description.

I was especially amused that one of the stories called 'Magic Sperm', had been rejected by the editor of Punch, Mr MacIntosh's fellow-Scotsman Peter McKay on the grounds that its title would cause offence.

In this book he recounts with the same good humour and the same descriptive power his experiences in the 'White Man's Grave'. I can warmly recommend it.

Chapter 1
TRAVELLER IN AN ANTIQUE LAND

'Take care and beware the Bight of Benin;
There's ten comes out for twenty goes in.'

The first thing you notice is the heat. You expect heat in the tropics, but this is something else. This is heat such as you have never known before, and it is like no heat you are ever likely to encounter anywhere else. It is a far cry from the sort of heat you have just left – the drowsy, clean heat of an English springtime, with the gentle fragrances of meadowsweet and clover lingering in the evening air. Nor can it be compared to the heat of the Costa Brava, the sort of heat that is born of Mediterranean skies and silver sands and placid seas. It is not even the heat of the open savannahs fringing the great desert you have just flown over – the shimmering, relentless heat that turns every scrubby bush and blade of grass to a drab and uniform beige; a glare of heat that reflects from the white gowns of tall Fulani herdsmen as they chivvy their cattle along endless dusty trails to coastal markets, and dazzles the eyes with its hurting fierceness.

This heat is like none of those. This heat is savage and smothers you in its clammy embrace the moment you step out of the plane, cloying, suffocating in its viscous intensity. You try to breathe in deeply and your lungs fill, not with cool draughts of civilized air, but with some alien mixture that seems to have the consistency of thin, warm porridge.

And it smells. You have only just arrived, but already the coolness of the plane interior is a fast-fading memory. You are on the tarmac of an international airport but already you are aware of the hot wet aroma of the bush all around you, an unforgettable mishmash of olfactory delights in which elderly socks and mouldering cabbage leaves vie with each other for pre-eminence. Now you know what the first gilled horror ever to set foot on land must have inhaled when it crawled out of the primordial sea to take its first tentative sniff of the earth's virgin air.

I picked up my bag and began to walk to the customs shed. A lizard shot from under my feet and scuttled across the tarmac. It stopped abruptly about five yards away and looked at me over its shoulder. It was about a foot long, with a slate-blue back and a bright orange head. It had a long, tapering tail ringed with dull orange and white hoops and it did manic press-ups on the blistering tar as it studied me. It looked like a dragon in miniature.

A movement beyond it caught the corner of my eye and I looked up in time to see another lizard launch itself from the roof of one of the airport buildings. It sailed through the air like a doomed hang-glider to land with a resounding splat on its belly 12 feet below. Apparently unharmed, it immediately engaged in ferocious combat with the first lizard, attacking it for no other apparent reason than to pass the time of day. I looked up at the roof from where it had thrown itself. There were legions of lizards up there, every square yard of the asbestos sheeting covered with them, sunning themselves. Some were of the size and colour of the two now scrapping in front of me, but, from their much smaller size and sombre hue, it was obvious that the majority were female. Two of those clung to the wall of the shed, watching with feigned disinterest the fracas raging below them, but the others lay torpid on the baking roof, eyes heavy-lidded, dreaming lizard dreams, awaiting the cool of the evening and the bonanza of insects that the lengthening shadows would bring within their reach.

Lizards and smells and sweltering heat. Little did I think at that moment that this would be my life for the next quarter of a century.

The Africa of those days was still in the grip of colonialism, but it was the grip of a tired and feeble old man. A new Africa was rising, and this Africa was vibrant and raucous and challenging. This Africa had no time for tired old men. She was in too much of a hurry.

Nothing exemplified this fact more than Lagos. In the midst of this vast and awful slum of rusting corrugated iron – this gigantic, sprawling, incredibly ugly shanty town – a rash of almost equally ugly concrete edifices was sprouting. Office blocks, hotels, restaurants and supermarkets in various stages of completion and incompletion were scattered higgledy-piggledy among the old traditional trading stores; stores that still sold bolts of cloth from Manchester, machetes made in Birmingham and sardines canned in Portugal, much in the way that they had been doing for the past hundred years and more. Jammed in between them and into every conceivable cranny of space were tiny shacks that would offer to sell you anything from a cure for craw-craw to a woman for the night. The stench from the open sewers that meandered stickily throughout this architectural nightmare was quite indescribable.

The racket stupefied the senses. Maniacal taxi drivers roared past at suicidal speeds, their horns honking and hooting and blaring without cessation. Wireless sets and gramophones blasted out African highlife music to the very heavens, market mammies kept up a constant barrage of vituperation at their children from roadside stalls and goats blatted plaintively in every doorway.

The night, I was soon to find, was even worse. Not only were the normal daytime noises cranked up a decibel or two by everyone and everything making them; they were boosted by the considerable vocal powers of one of the city's most enduring inhabitants. The Nigerian cockerel must surely be the noisiest of its ilk, and Lagos, in those days, must have been blessed with more cockerels per acre than any other city in the whole of Africa. They suffered from chronic insomnia and all of them seemed determined to ensure that every living creature in the city should suffer along with them. They crowed throughout the long, long night in a thousand different sharps and flats. Battle-hardened veterans hurled their hoarse insults far into the darkness from unseen eminences. Lusty young pretenders, at the peak of their vocal powers if not yet of their sexual prowesses, replied from the safety of distant rooftops, and adolescents squawked their timorous unfinished symphonies from their hiding places among the crumbling shacks.

It was utter bedlam. Urban life in West Africa is bedlam wherever you go, but for sheer cacophonous horror the Lagos of those days just had to be in a class of its own.

I stayed the first couple of nights in a government rest house on the outskirts of town. In contrast to the noisome squalor outside, the house was neat and clean. The mahogany floor shone with the gloss that can only be achieved by constant hand polishing and crisp white linen adorned the dining room tables. A large ceiling fan rotated slowly with a monotonous CHUNK . . . CHUNK . . . CHUNK . . . sound as it shunted the hot air lethargically around the room.

A steward appeared out of nowhere. He was magnificently attired. The brass buttons on his immaculately ironed, pristine white uniform positively glowed, and the emerald flashes on the epaulettes proclaimed his authority to all who entered the rest house portals.

There was only one other guest, an old Coaster with a BBC accent and skin of the colour and texture of Dead Sea scrolls. He sat at a table in the corner with a bottle of imported beer before him. Even before he spoke I could sense the aura of jaded cynicism that enveloped him. He asked me what I was doing in this God-forsaken country. 'I'm a forester,' I replied noncommittally.

He digested this piece of information in silence and I joined him at his table. He was the Lagos-based manager of an international shipping line, he informed me, and he was staying at this rest house while his own home on the European reservation was being renovated. He had been 15 years on the Coast, and he had never ventured outside Lagos. Nor had he any intention of doing so, he declared emphatically. 'Enough snakes and rats in this bloody town without going to bush to look for them!' he said sourly.

He hated Africa and its people, he told me, but he would soldier on for as long as he could because the money was good. He needed the cash − his three children were at expensive boarding schools in England. His wife rarely came out to the Coast now, mainly because she had an even greater aversion to Africa than he had. He saw all of them at the end of every tour when he returned to England − two months of familial duty every couple of years or so. He still had six months of his present tour to complete before his next leave was due and he could hardly wait. Every morning when he came down to breakfast, he told me, he took out his pen and scored off the previous day's date on the rest house calendar. This had been his daily ritual for the past 15 years, and it was the thing that he most looked forward to in the whole day. Right now, he informed me proudly, he could tell me exactly how many days remained before he next set sail for England.

Long before I managed to excuse myself from his company much later that evening, my original euphoria at finding myself in Africa had vanished to be replaced by a lowering depression. I glanced back from the doorway as I left the room. He was sitting there just as I had left him, umpteenth drink raised to his lips. The skin of his face was ochre-coloured in the electric light and his watery, malarial eyes stared unseeingly at the opposite wall.

I closed the door quietly behind me. As I walked off to my room the ponderous CHUNK . . . CHUNK . . . CHUNK . . . of the ceiling fan echoed hollowly behind me – a metronome tolling its requiem over the living dead.

My work took me far from the ghettos and human tragedies of Lagos. Indeed, I reflected thankfully, I was unlikely to set foot in Lagos again for a long time. As my transport jolted its way up the red laterite track through the swamps to the north of the city, my gloom swiftly dissipated. I was heading for West Africa's fabled rainforests and I knew that I was only a day's drive from the beginning of the greatest experience of my life.

I still remember how the air seemed to crackle with excitement on that first morning – excitement, expectancy and a million unformed questions. This was high adventure. But there was more to it than that. Much more. There was a strange feeling within me now, a feeling I had never known before, one which could not be explained away as being a mere quickening of the pulse at the thought of impending adventure. I had this inexplicable feeling of contentment, of serenity, a feeling almost of destiny fulfilled already. I do not recall having any thoughts of sadness on that morning about having left home and family behind me. I can remember only this tremendous elation, this strange feeling that, on the contrary, home was where I was going right now.

It was an odd sensation, because this land could not possibly have differed more from the land of my birth. I was born in Scotland of Highland parents. My father was a woodcutter. He was a good one, too, and much sought after by the many timber outfits scattered around the Scotland of his time. He was, as a result, on the move a lot. He felled larch for the masts of the *Cutty Sark* on the precipitous slopes of the Ross and Cromarty glens, and he felled ash and Scots pine for the war effort in the gentler climes and terrain of Galloway. He usually lived in bothies during the week, returning home to us at weekends. When his work took him too far from home, we simply moved house to be near to him.

A Highland child was as great a curiosity in rural Galloway in those days as a Cherokee Indian might have been. With my father away from home so much it was perhaps inevitable that I should attach myself firmly to my Hebridean grandfather. This was to create certain problems when I went to school in Wigtownshire to begin my formal education. My grandfather spoke no English worth mentioning, with the result that, while my knowledge of Gaelic was such that I was even able to read in that ancient language by the time I was five years of age, I might as well have been speaking Tocharian insofar as the pupils of Garlieston Primary School were concerned. Their playground conversations were carried out in a form of Broad Scots virtually incomprehensible to all but Gallovidians, while I could barely manage half-a-dozen words of even the basic English taught within the school building.

I learned fast. Children do, especially when forced by circumstance to live among strangers. The ugly duckling syndrome has particular application to children. Change, or be ostracized, was the norm even in those less cruel times. Inside school I learned standard English, while outside school I learned to get my tongue around the harsh gutturals of the 'Galloway-Irish' dialect. Under the tutelage of my grandfather I continued to read Gaelic by night. Of more consequence from my point of view, however, was the fact that I learned from my father and grandfather an appreciation of wild things and wild places. The pounding of stormy seas against black rocks on the Cruggleton shore and the wind soughing through the tall elms of the Pouton wood in the early days of spring gave a special sort of peace that would enfold my body like a silken quilt when I was far from the haunts of man.

Lonely places, remote woodlands, have always fascinated me. Thoreau wrote: 'I have never found a companion that was so companionable as solitude.' It was a sentiment that might have been written for me.

It was inevitable, I suppose, that I should take up forestry as a career. My father had been a woodsman all his life and the woods were in my blood. I loved their scents and sounds: the turpentine fragrance of the pines on a hot summer's day, and the welcoming song of the chaffinch ringing out through the treetops as I climbed over the drystone dyke to get into the old wood at the top of the hill.

What is less easy to explain was my reason for wanting to leave such tranquillity behind me. Why this inexplicable longing to go to the savage forests of tropical Africa, a longing I remember experiencing even in primary school? Had I read something somewhere that had stirred the childish imagination? A *Boy's Own Paper* adventure story, perhaps? Or had my grandfather or my father told me some tale of this land of mystery and juju that had enraptured me? If so, I cannot remember it now. I only know that this strange compulsion had been with me since ever I can remember. 'Donald's going to Africa, to bring a monkey back with him . . .' are two lines from a song that a Highland uncle invented about me when I was six years of age, so it must have been apparent to all and sundry even then in which part of the world lay my fantasies.

After leaving school I worked for a time with the Forestry Commission in the ancient forest of Kilsture, before being posted to the mountains of Argyll for a two-year stint at a forestry school. When I graduated and was asked to specify whether I wanted a career in forestry within the United Kingdom, there could have been but one answer. My eyes lit upon the 'Overseas Vacancies' pamphlet on the interviewer's desk in front of me, and it seemed as though the Almighty Himself was trying to tell me something. A forester was required for West Africa, and the 'White Man's Grave' never had a more eager recruit.

*   *   *

If Lagos was in the throes of a new dawn, the people outside the city boundaries appeared to be blissfully unaware of the fact. Time, it seemed, stood still here. Everywhere I looked, I saw Africa as she had always been. A woman walked sedately along the roadside as her forebears had done for centuries past, a huge pan piled high with market produce balanced perfectly on her head, while behind her in single file walked her six children in order of size, tallest to the front and smallest at the rear. Each carried a pan on his or her head, the pans being graduated in size according to the size of the individual child, with each pan filled with either fruit or vegetables. The tiny, naked tot at the end, I noted, had a little bowl on his head containing a single avocado. To the rear of this procession came papa, looking stately in his long blue robes. All that this Great Man deigned to carry was one black umbrella, which he had neatly rolled up and placed on his head.

A man squatted by the roadside, urinating. He straightened up when he heard the approach of our vehicle. He turned to face us, a broad grin on his face. He waved animatedly, his other hand holding his penis, still peeing away, quite unabashed. A little further on, under a stumpy, strange-looking palm tree fringing the swamps, a group of old men were gathered, drinking something from a large brown calabash.

The road was terrible, a corrugated, rutted nightmare full of deep potholes. The rains were long since over, but nothing appeared to have been done to repair the damage to the road surface. The wrecks of smashed and burned out vehicles were strewn everywhere, most of them lying, festooned with liana, in the surrounding swamps but many left scattered along the sides of the road. About 20 miles further on I came upon a broken down grader, its yellow coat of paint just barely visible here and there beneath its covering of red laterite dust. It had obviously been there since at least the previous dry season. Just beyond it a small bridge had been washed away and a very rough causeway of dirt and sticks crossed the now-dry bed of the stream it had once spanned.

We were still heading north. Our surroundings were less swampy now and oil palms were becoming more frequent along the road verges, their stiffly straight black trunks making them less aesthetic to the eye than the sinuous lime-green grace of the coconut palms I had seen around the coastline. Now we began to meet women carrying huge, heavy-looking bunches of shiny, black-and-carmine palm fruit on their heads, with a machete perched on top of the load. Often they would have tiny babies slung on their backs, with only the little round heads visible above the swathes of brightly coloured cloth wrapped around them.

The women never failed to smile as our vehicle passed, their teeth sparkling the purest of white in the sun. Despite their enormous loads, they would often stop to wave at us as we passed them in a cloud of dust. A colossal tree a little way in off the road caught my eye. I told the driver to stop. A well-worn path led from the road through what I recognized as being a small grove of cocoa trees. The giant tree, silver-barked, immensely cylindrical and ruler straight, towered some 200 feet or more above the cocoa. I walked down the path towards it, marvelling at it, wondering what it was, thinking how my father, who loved trees, would have enjoyed this moment. Its massive buttresses spread in all directions through the cocoa and extended high up the bole.

A very old man hobbled along the path towards me, grinning widely. 'Wel-i-come, massa. Wel-i-come!' I tried to strike up a conversation with him by asking his name, where he had come from, what work he did – all sorts of banal questions – but he just kept on grinning foolishly at me, obviously not understanding a single word I was saying. Finally, I pointed to the tree and said: 'This tree. You know it?'

That seemed to register with him, all right. His grin became even broader, threatening to split his face in two: 'Yassah, massa. I know am good.'

I waited, while the old man stood before me, just grinning disconcertingly into my face. 'Well,' I said, enunciating my words carefully so that he could not fail to understand me, 'What is it, then? The English name for this tree?'

The grin vanished. He looked perplexed, embarrassed even. He turned to face the tree, scratching his grizzled woolly pate, shuffling uneasily. He looked the tree up and down, peering at the crown high above us, like an aged, dotty scientist trying to stir a fading memory into action to recall a particularly difficult botanical name for some obscure plant. Finally, like a 200-watt bulb suddenly lighting up in a 40-watt container, it dawned on him. He turned to me delightedly: 'I remember now, massa,' he said. 'I remember.'

I waited patiently.

'Dem callam in h-English, massa . . .'

'Yes?'

'Na "Useless Tree", massa. That is what dem callem. Na "Useless Tree",' he cried triumphantly.

I walked back to my vehicle, content. Whatever misgivings I had had remaining about this strange, hot, primitive land before this meeting had vanished completely. Now I knew for sure that my stay here was going to be long and entertaining.

Chapter 2
WHISPERS FROM THE PAST

Although it was only after the end of World War II that the great timber boom of the Coast managed to build up a real head of steam, things had been stirring in the undergrowth long before that. In fact, even before the onset of World War I it had been obvious to anyone with half an eye that the true mahoganies, the *Swietenias* of the Caribbean and tropical America, were in a state of terminal decline. The moguls of the rapidly expanding European furniture trade began to cast their nets around frantically, trawling the forests of the world for anything that even remotely resembled mahogany. And, as it became increasingly obvious that acceptable substitutes were few and far between, their attention began to focus on a land not all that far from home, a land known only to a few eccentric explorers, a land of mystery and sinister legend and death. They took their first long, speculative look at the land already known to much of the civilized world as 'The White Man's Grave'.

Like many another great event in history, the exploitation of the rainforests of West Africa had started innocently enough. Even as far back as the early years of the 19th century a few adventurers had noted the potential of the Coast as a possible source of timber. But it had been, at best, a drowsy sort of interest. Small parcels of ebony and camwood had been shipped in dribs and drabs through the turbulent seas of the Bay of Biscay to the ports of England and the Continent, but that was about as far as it went. These were the traditional, proven species and, with timber in plentiful supply everywhere else in the world, sawmillers felt no need to experiment with new and exotic timbers as yet. It is true that every now and then some far-sighted entrepreneur would have a rush of blood to the head and slip into those shipments a few logs of some species that no one had ever heard of before, but these would turn out to be species that, more often than not, would be allowed to vanish back into the obscurity from whence they had originated after they had succeeded in shattering the teeth of every saw in the mills to which they had been sent for cutting.

In fact, it was the density and hardness of most of these West African species that was one of the major reasons why the timber resources of that part of the world had been left in peace for so long. There were few timber merchants who were prepared to put their health and wealth on the line in trying to establish logging companies in unchartered tropical swamps that produced timber of such extreme hardness that it ruined their equipment in their attempts to saw it. This timber was of such granite toughness that even nails could not be hammered into it.

Mind you, as might have been expected, much of this exotic timber was pretty durable stuff. The wood cells were often full of silica and, if you ever did manage to render the logs into plank form, you could rest assured that the planks would still be around long after you yourself had departed to a hopefully better world.

One species called *Oldfieldia* was a typical example. A few logs were exported to England in the late 1820s and, after playing the predicted havoc with many an expensive saw, they were finally reduced to planks and put to use as decking in a naval frigate. More than a hundred years later, when the rest of the ship had mouldered to dust at its final mooring, the decking was still as good as new.

But these were very sporadic shipments and they were, for the most part, highly experimental by nature. There were, indeed, years when very little timber of any kind left the shores of the Coast. In the early years of the 20th century the main West African export centred around the fruit of the oil palm, or *Elaeis guineensis*, to give it its botanical name. This was very much in demand in Europe for the making of margarine and soap, and it was shipped in both kernel and oil form.

Also in great demand at that time was the fruit of the shea-butter tree (*Butyrospermum parkii*), which was used in the making of chocolate cream. This was a squat, branchy tree, rather like a hedgerow oak in appearance, which was common in the savannah parkland just to the north of the rainforest belt. At the end of each dry season it produced a fruit something like a wild green plum in size and shape. Inside this was a small, glossy brown nut, from which the Africans extracted a cooking oil by prolonged boiling. Generally it would be exported in nut form, but sometimes it would be shipped in solidified slabs of 'butter' – the method by which it was stored for domestic use by the natives.

Records for 1908 show that, in addition to the aforementioned products, Liberia exported over seven million pounds of piassava (palm fibre used in the making of ropes and brooms), one-and-a-half million pounds of coffee beans and 15,000 pounds of ivory during that particular year, while records of shipments from Nigeria and the Gambia for the same period show, intriguingly, that each of those countries exported nearly 300 tons of beeswax. During this period only three countries – Ivory Coast, Cameroon and Gold Coast – are shown as having exported any timber at all, and even then the amounts were insignificant.

Things hotted up a little, timber-wise, in the years immediately preceding World War I, particularly insofar as Germany and Britain were concerned. In 1913 the Germans exported 18,000 tons of logs, taken from 23 different species, from Cameroon, and the British shipped around 80,000 tons of timber in log form from Nigeria. Significantly, the British cargo was all shipped under the classification of 'mahogany'. The furniture moguls had found their substitute.

And a very good substitute they had found too. Or rather, substitutes, for the new 'mahogany' consisted of eight separate species in all, ranging from the much-sought-after *Khaya ivorensis*, or lagoswood, to the colossus with the jaw-breaking scientific name, *Entandrophragma cylindricum*, or sapelewood. None of them were mahoganies in the true sense of the word, but they were very closely related to the Caribbean originals. To all but the fussiest of connoisseurs they looked every bit as good as – if not better than – the true mahogany. Their timbers had a warmth and a sheen and a fragrance that can only be found in the most mature and venerable of trees and the most ancient of species. They were often figured with beautiful whorls and stripes and patterns never to be seen in timbers taken from the regimental plantations of man. The trees were invariably of good diameter, ruler-straight of trunk and totally free of branches right up to the crown and these factors made them ideally suited to the sawmills of the day. Nor were these new 'mahoganies' particularly difficult to work with. Most of them were considerably easier to saw than English oak and elm. Most important of all, they were there in the White Man's Grave in seemingly limitless quantities. All that was needed was the wherewithal and the technical know-how to get them out.

Although it would be another 40 years before all these tentative gropings and probings at the portals of West Africa's virgin forests were to degenerate into a full-scale gang rape, those years of trial and error immediately prior to, and immediately following, World War 1 were significant. The mahoganies of the Coast has passed their first big test on the European markets and things would never be quite the same again for those from whose lands they had been taken.

But what was the black man, the real owner of these forests, doing while all this activity was taking place? The answer to that question was: not much that he hadn't been doing for donkey's years before the coming of the white man. The white stranger's preoccupation with hacking down the largest and finest of the trees growing in the endless forests of the Coast bothered the real inhabitants not one jot. For a few of the coastal tribes, the arrival of the white timber man was even a blessing. He provided employment, and if the wages he paid were a pittance, it was better than having no money at all. 'Half-bread better pass no bread' was a Coast saying even in those days. The white man was not entering into direct competition with the black man for his day-to-day requirements from the forest, was he? His timber needs were quite different – he wanted trees of a kind and an enormity of size that the black man couldn't be bothered with. Besides, there was enough for everyone, wasn't there?

It was a pretty harmonious relationship. The black man of the Coast was a tolerant and easy-going character. So long as the sun shone in the sky during the dry season and the rain came down each year as scheduled to fatten his yams, and so long as he had no one firing poisoned arrows at his backside at any given moment, he had not a care in the world. The great environmental beastie was still several decades away from rearing its green and mournful head above the horizon and no one, black or white, spent too much time fretting about global warming and holes in the ozone layer back in those days.

So the lifestyle of the forest indigène changed little, if at all. He felled the small, straight-stemmed abura of the wetlands for the making of doors and beams and rafters for his mud huts, and he poled his canoe through the brackish waters of the coastal swamps in search of white mangrove to burn for the manufacture of his bush salt. On the drier slopes of the inland forests he carved talking-drums from the resonant wood of the luminous-barked cordia tree, and on the edges of forest clearings he found the claret-red camwood and the bright yellow, fragrant yaru wood for the making of his dyes.

He used the bark of many different species of tree, too, and for a variety of purposes. Often these purposes had much to do with the masculine libido. An infusion of the bark of the gigantic okan, hardest of all African timbers, was said to guarantee the production of male progeny each time he performed, and palm wine containing pieces of bark from the grotesque tala tree, or *Sacoglottis gabonensis*, was said to bless the man drinking it with prodigious sexual powers '. . . 10 women one night, or one women 10 times in one night . . .' I was repeatedly assured in more than one country along the Coast by men whose practical knowledge of the subject I had no reason to doubt.

I often wondered if those early timber barons, who had so little success in their attempts to introduce the heavy, dark-red timber of the tala tree to the markets of the world, had in fact been exporting the wrong part of it.

Canoe making was always a major industry on the Coast, and the men who fashioned those dug-out canoes were artisans of the highest calibre. Various tree species were used, and the type of timber favoured seemed to depend on the sort of conditions in which it was meant to be used. The coastal tribes seemed to prefer the heavier and more durable species, while tribes from drier hinterland areas seemed to favour the lighter – albeit less durable – species.

The selected tree would be felled at the waterside, then crosscut to the desired length. The two sides were then squared off with adzes, while an axeman hacked out a deep, narrow groove along the length of the log. While he was doing so, wooden staves would be fixed firmly into the groove to keep it open. At the same time, another adzeman would be shaping the bow and stern.

When the canoe had taken shape, dry palm branches would then be placed on the ground around it, and cross pieces prepared and laid across the canoe at the point where they were to be positioned as thwarts in the finished article. Opposite each of those, long, flexible green stakes were hammered into the ground, to be used as levers over the canoe. The palms were then set on fire around the area of each thwart, starting at the bow end. The heat made the timber expand, opening the canoe, at which point the workers would haul the lever down hard over the canoe, opening it wide enough to allow the thwarts to be jammed inside. The process would be repeated along the length of the canoe until each thwart was firmly in place.

These canoes were remarkable works of art and they would last for many years. They were very wobbly, and they took some getting used to. One of my better moments on the Coast was of witnessing a rather grand young varsity rowing blue stepping into his first dug-out canoe with the careless insouciance that one might expect from chaps of such exalted status. A split second later he was in ten feet of the muddiest water in the whole of West Africa, new palm-beach suit and all, among the eels and the catfish, with the canoe upside down on top of him. He was eventually gaffed by an old Ijaw waterman, whose ribald running commentary displayed a disgraceful lack of respect for his betters and did no credit at all to his race.

Flattening trees en masse was not a thing the forest native did by choice. There was seldom any need to. Apart from the clearing of the occasional patch of ground for his yams' and his rice, his needs were pretty basic. He felled the occasional large tree to pitsaw into planks, but for the most part he left them alone. For him, the real value of trees lay in the fact that they provided cover for the animals he hunted and they provided food for himself and his family. He sent his wives and children into the forest to gather the delectable nuts of the aspen-like iku tree and the sprawling okwe vine. The walnut-like nuts of the small coula tree were gathered by the sackful for sale and barter – that is, if the chimpanzees had not got at them first. The mighty makore tree produced an annual bonanza of mango-like fruit. These were gathered and boiled to extract their oil, and it was a cooking oil of a clarity and delicacy that cannot be bettered by any of the varieties on sale in the supermarkets of today.

In the ebony forests of Liberia and Nigeria the grubs of the goliath beetle were to be found among the rotting debris of the forest floor. They were about three inches long and about half an inch fat and they were of an odd, rather off-putting, translucent white hue, like the belly of a certain kind of garden slug. Some tribes ate them alive, nipping off the black, chitinous heads with their teeth and squeezing the body contents into their mouths as one would squeeze the contents from a tube of toothpaste. My own tastes being much more refined and civilized, I could never bring myself to do this. I preferred them well done in palm oil.

There is no question that the ordinary native of the bush considered the palm tree to be the most valuable tree in West Africa. He had every reason to do so. The palm tree is one of the wonders of nature. It is not really a timber tree at all, though the timber of one tree, the fan palm, is hard and durable and most decorative, being of a beautiful silvery-grey hue, with numerous chocolaty-purple fibre streaks. The fan palm is very occasionally used as a building timber, but it is essentially a tree of the open spaces and is rarely to be encountered in the depths of the forest.

There are, in fact, about 15 different varieties of palm to be found throughout West Africa, and all of them are important in one way or another. Some, such as the rattan and the roofing palm, are used extensively in house building activities, while others, such as the king palm and the wild date, are used in medicine and juju rituals. But none are as important as the oil palm. The oil palm is the belly of the Coast.

It is also the most common of all palms. It is indigenous to West Africa and it is to be found just about everywhere. It is particularly noticeable around farms and villages, but even in the most remote parts of the forest one will come across tall, gangly specimens, which are the progeny of nuts dropped by monkeys and parrots decades earlier. Inside the gloom of the forest the oil palm will grow to 80 feet high, unlike the thicker stemmed trees of the open farmlands which rarely exceed 30 feet in height but which nevertheless produce by far the greater quantity of fruit.

Oil palms start fruiting when they are about five years of age and will often continue to bear fruit until they are nearing their centenary. The glossy, black-tipped, carmine fruit is roughly the size of a damson and it consists of a small kernel surrounded by a thick, hard shell and a tough, stringy pericarp. The fruits are packed tightly together in a large clump the same shape as − but slightly larger than − a rugby football. These bunches are to be found at the top of the tree, where the fronds begin to arc out from the trunk. The immature fruits are soft and sweet and absolutely delicious, but the mature ones are so stone hard as to be quite inedible to anything with teeth and jaws less powerful than those of the average male silverback gorilla. (Or so I thought until the first time I saw my own workers crunching their way through them with relish.)

To reach the fruit the collector first makes a strong, thick rope of liana, one end of which he loops round the stem of the palm tree and the other around his waist. Bracing his back against the rope and his feet against the bole, he hoists himself up the tree, step by step, to the crown. With a large chisel-shaped piece of iron, he severs the stalks of the bunches and allows them to drop to the ground. Having done this, his task is over − it is up to his wives and children to carry the bunches home for him.

The oil is extracted by steaming the fruit in a large pot over an open fire until it softens. Then the hot, fibrous pulp is pounded to mush in mortars or – when it is being processed in large quantities – dumped in a long trough of weathered, beaten clay with flat stones and old palm nuts lining the bottom of it. Water is then poured into this trough and the fruit is tramped underfoot for hours on end. (This task is always performed by the women.) As the ochre-coloured, fatty oil rises to the surface of the water, it is scooped out by the children in attendance and put into a clean pot to boil. When it has been boiling for an hour or so, it is strained to remove impurities.

The finished product is, quite simply, ambrosia. It is supreme among edible oils, and the glow of its amber-red richness proclaims its supremacy to you the moment you first set eyes on it. It is a glow that comes straight from the heart of it, and it goes straight to the heart of you. No man can call himself a gourmet until he has sampled 'palm oil chop' cooked over an open fire by one of those wonderful women of the forest far from the realm of the microwave.

Palm oil chop is peculiar to West Africa. There is nothing quite like it anywhere else in the world. Ask any black women of the Coast and she will tell you that the oil palm is the king of all palms. Here, as in many other things, she differs from her consort. For him, the tombo palm is the monarch of all palm trees.

If the oil palm is the woman's tree, then the tombo tree is the living soul of the African male. This is the palm wine tree, or *Raphia vinifera*, for those interested in such matters, though I doubt if many of those with whom I shared a calabash or two over the years cared much what the scientists called it.

The tombo palm grows at its best on the edge of freshwater swamps. It will grow in the shadows of the rainforest giants, but it will not do so happily, and in these conditions it will not produce palm wine worth drinking. It likes to see the sun, but it does not mind being surrounded by its own kind. It is not a tall tree – it is seldom more than 12 feet in height – and it has the longest fronds of any of the African palms, sometimes up to 50 feet long. Partly because of this, it has a rather untidy look compared to the other palms, a sort of straggly-haired, bohemian look, that fits in cosily with the tangles of thorns and ferns and creepers that invariably surround it. Under ideal conditions it will produce astonishing quantities of wine; I have known trees to supply a steady, two large calabashes full-to-the-brim-with-wine every 24 hours for three weeks. The quality of the wine varies very considerably and no one knows why this should be so – it is not uncommon to have a 'good' tree growing right beside a 'bad' tree, in exactly the same ground conditions and of the same height and appearance.

The tapper climbs the tree to the point where the fronds begin to radiate from the main stem and he chisels a hole into the trunk to release the sap. He then fixes a calabash over the aperture, covering the point of contact with a wrapping of leaves to keep out flies and other suicidal insects – a precautionary measure not always successful. Every morning and every evening the calabash is removed and replaced until the wine flow eventually peters out.

The wine is creamy white in colour. When fresh, it is thin and foamy, with a sweet but sharp taste. At this stage it is most pleasant and refreshing and not very alcoholic at all. If kept for a day or so it begins to ferment, becoming bitter to the taste and – when taken even in relatively small quantity – quite intoxicating.

Palm wine is very much an acquired taste, and very few whites enjoy it on their first encounter with it. The warm flouriness of the stuff and the discovery (alas, often too late to be of much practical use to the drinker) that corpses of drowned flies, beetles, spiders and maggots tend to feature prominently in any calabash of palm wine, all combine to discourage the novitiate tippler. I suppose that I, too, went through this phase of initial revulsion, but within a short space of time I became quite fond of the stuff. Palm wine drinking in the bush is as much a social thing as it is a cheap way of getting mildly drunk, and it is no small honour to be invited by a wine tapper to come with him to his 'special' tree to pass the time of day with him.

Some time in the latter part of the 1960s I was sitting by the edge of a swamp drinking palm wine with an old hunter friend called, somewhat mysteriously, Two-At-One-Time. It had been many years since we had last met and the white man with his machines had not, at that time, reached those great forests in which Two-At-One-Time had been born and raised. Now, a logging road cut through the area and a long wooden bridge spanned the river about 100 yards upstream from where we sat. Some bridge repairs were under way, with the result that a long queue of timber lorries, loaded high with massive logs, were stuck on the other side of the bridge waiting to cross.

I counted the trucks. Eight in all, and each, I estimated, carrying about 25 tons of timber. I turned to Two-At-One-Time.

'How long have those lorries been waiting there?'

'About two hours,' he replied.

'And when will they be back for more?' I asked.

'Tomorrow,' he said. 'They come here every day. Why do you ask?'

I did not answer him immediately. I was thinking. Two hundred tons of logs. And two hundred tons of logs tomorrow. And the next day. And the next. It was a lot of timber.

'What will happen to you and your people,' I said at length, 'When all your trees have gone? When these white people have gone back to their own land and taken all your bush with them?'

He thought about this for a little, but I could see that it was not a subject that bothered him unduly. He shrugged and grinned. 'There will always be forest in Africa,' he said. Then, with true African logic, he continued: 'In any case, that is for tomorrow. And tomorrow is another day.'

He reached for the calabash again and refilled his cup. He handed the calabash over to me. 'Anyway,' he said, 'they can take all they want. It won't bother you and me. So long as they leave our tombo trees alone.'

I poured myself some more wine. A drowned fruit-fly floated to the surface in my cup, its large pink goggly eyes staring accusingly up at me. I fished it out with my finger and lifted the cup to my mouth.

'I suppose you're right,' I said.

Chapter 3
THE AGE OF INNOCENCE

The road to hell is paved with good intentions, and the Colonial Office could never have been accused of being short of good intentions. One of their more laudable schemes, among a host of singularly daft wheezes, has been the formation of the Colonial Forestry Department. Its aims were two-fold. Firstly, to establish some sort of control over the exploitation of the vast tracts of forest to be found in most of Britain's colonies, and secondly, to establish planting and regeneration programmes within those countries. The thoughts behind those aims were, of course, as pure as the driven snow. No one would ever have been so ungenerous as to suggest that they had anything to do with the very considerable financial benefits Britain would derive from the exploitation of those forest resources.

It was not, however, until the early years of the 20th century that they got themselves organized in the White Man's Grave. Those years immediately prior to – and following – the Great War saw the establishment of forestry departments all along the Coast. Even countries such as Togo and Sierra Leone, places that have never caught the imagination of the average logging man insofar as forest exploitation is concerned, began to implement ambitious planting programmes, experimenting with plantations of indigenous species like sasswood in mixture with foreign ones such as Burmese teak. Nigeria, with its enormous timber resources, led the way in its attempts to set up a system of felling controls. The colonial government of the day established a system of forest reserves, vast areas of high forest ranging from 50 to several hundred square miles in extent, which would be protected from local shifting cultivation and which would be under the jurisdiction of the government forestry department. Felling within those reserves would only be granted to reputable timber companies on licence, and then only under the strictest of conditions. One of these conditions was that only a specified area would be felled each year, and the area granted for felling usually amounted to no more than a one-hundredth portion of the total area of the forest reserve in question. Thus, in a reserve totalling 100 square miles, a one-square-mile block of forest per year would be allowed for felling, after which the block would be handed back to the forestry department by the concessionaire for future replanting and regeneration purposes. In this way, it was hoped, the perpetuity of the forest would be guaranteed.

Various fees and royalties would be paid by the logging operatives for the privilege of felling within those reserves. Back in the early 1900s these ranged from around £3 sterling per tree for the more prized *Khaya* mahoganies, to a nominal fee of sixpence per tree for such rarely used species as mangrove and *Anogeissus*, the chew-stick tree.

With various small modifications and substantial price hikes from time to time over the years to meet the demands of improved technology, this, basically, was the system that operated in West African forests right throughout the first half of the 20th century.

There was, of course, a bit more to it than that. Much more, in fact. Logging companies could not just charge in and start flattening trees wherever they wanted even though the forest was theirs on paper. The forest reserve had to be properly surveyed, and responsibility for doing so was the operative's. Everything from the smallest rock outcrop to the tiniest rivulet had to be plotted in minute detail on large-scale maps. Each tree whose bole measured over four feet in girth at breast height had to be recorded by species and girth on the same maps. All this had to be done by the concessionaire long in advance of felling and, indeed, copies of those maps had to be in the hands of the government forestry people before permission to fell would even be considered by them.

It was a laborious, time-consuming, and – for the concessionaire – costly process. But it paid dividends in the end, particularly for the really big operatives. The maps showed them at a glance where the valuable stands of timber were, and they also showed the swamps and other hazards to be avoided in getting their timber out.

For a youngster such as myself, given the task of tree identification and enumeration far ahead of the logging crews after World War II, it was to prove the ideal introduction to life in the rainforests in tropical Africa.

At the time of my arrival in West Africa, timber companies had done little that could have upset any but the most far-sighted of conservation visionaries. Logging techniques were still almost as primitive as in the days when pitsawyers supplied Albert Schweitzer with planks for his hospital in Gabon back in the early days of the century. Tropical logging on the Coast was still in its nappies. This was partly because the necessary mechanical backing was virtually non-existent outside the coastal towns. Felling was still done by axe and rafting was still the *modus operandi* for moving logs down through the delta creeks. This meant that much of the logging had to be concentrated around the creeks and waterways marking the Great River's approach to the Bight of Benin.

Contrary to popular modern belief colonial forestry officials could be quite tough with expatriate timber companies in those days if they stepped even marginally out of line. But it was not so easy controlling what often happened after the timber man had had his pound of flesh from his allocated portion of forest. All too often, far beyond the grasp of the law, the subsistence farmer would move in with his axe, machetes and his posse of wives, felling and burning all the small trees and undergrowth left behind by the logger. Where the future of the forest had once seemed so assured, now yams and cassava flourished. When a niche of this kind had been carved in the structure of the forest, the perpetrators would prove very difficult to evict. Within a surprisingly short time, after the farmer had told his myriad 'brothers' how easy it all was, the niche would have become an enclave of very considerable proportions.

Even in those days it was not always easy to balance the demands of hungry black families with the more lofty ideals propounded by white environmentalists who lived close to supermarkets. All the necessities for gracious living in comfortable homes were after all, far across the sea.

Not that any of us, black or white, gave too much thought to the future in those days. I think we all had a touch of the hedonist in us then. Life was for living to the full and right now, at that. Tomorrow could take care of itself. In any case, this bonanza of timber was inexhaustible and we, its exploiters, were merely rippling the surface of dear old Mother Africa's bottomless well . . .

While my own work generally kept me well away from the timber men, inevitably, because of the very nature of it, I would come into occasional contact with them. They were an interesting collection.

The Ibo axemen, in particular, were a breed unto themselves. They were short men, almost squat in appearance, with massive shoulders and arms. They were barrel-chested, and their waists and thighs were corded with muscle. Most of those I saw were quite bow-legged, as though the effort of carrying such massive frames was just too much for the knee joints to withstand.

They were marvellous axemen. They fascinated me. I can see them even as I write . . .

They stand — three to a tree when the tree is very big — high up on their stick platform, just above the point where the great sweeping buttresses meet the trunk. Their bodies are naked and gleam with sweat as they swing their axes. The heavy blades bite deep into the wood, sending a steady cataract of cedar-scented chunks tumbling to the ground beneath.

Sometimes it takes them a day, sometimes two days, to fell the tree, depending on its size. But the end, when it approaches, is always the same. Tendons close to the heart begin to shear, sending tiny crackling sounds rippling round the inside of the trunk like a tsunami wave. Axes are instantly laid down on the platform and the head axeman sends out his first warning halloos — a series of high-pitched yodels that reverberate throughout the forest canopy – which scatter flocks of green pigeons and parrots to the four points of the compass.

The fellers stand still now, listening. The whole forest is silent, expectant. A single loud crack comes from deep within the trunk and the headman is suddenly left on his own on the platform as his colleagues hurl their axes to the ground and scramble down the trestle supports after them.

The lone axeman picks up his axe and starts again, cautiously this time, administering the *coups de grâce*. He is, after all, the head axeman, and this is his right. He delivers his blows with steady, measured strokes, pausing between each one to listen to the tree 'talking' to him.

(Curious, I reflect now, how all of those old-time axemen maintained that the tree always 'talked' to them just before it fell. My father – one of the finest in Scotland – used to say the same.)

The end is near now. When it comes, it comes with a startling suddenness. The great heart bursts with a crack like a rifle shot and the executioner goes swinging down his trestle like a monkey to the safety of the ground below.

In awe, and with a numbing feeling of sadness, I watch as the stately, ancient giant shakes and shudders and groans in its death throes before finally giving up the ghost and wakening half of Africa as it thunders to the ground, smashing all before it.

The eerie silence that follows its fall, broken only by the steady patter of leaves and other debris from above, will live in my soul.

The massive boles were cut into manageable lengths by manually operated crosscut saws, which were long, cumbersome push-pull things that required the combined efforts of two men on each end, one grasping the handle and the other assisting him by pulling on a short length of rope attached to the handle. Crosscutting complete, the logs were then taken over by the hand-hauling gangs, whose task it was to skid the logs through the forest to the nearest waterside.

The hand-hauling was quite an operation. It was usually given out on contract, often to the chief of one of the waterside fishing villages. Rough skidding roads would be cut through the bush to the waterside and the logs skidded along those. Gangs of up to 60 men would be allotted to each log, depending on its size, and two ropes attached to its end. Occasionally rollers would be laid on the ground where conditions were unfavourable, but as often as not the log was simply hauled over the forest floor. The most important member of the team was the chap who did the least physical work himself – the contractor. His function was to spur on his labour with a continuous singing chant, one that would be echoed by his sweating workers as they strained on their ropes. It was his sole contribution to the whole business, but without this contribution it is doubtful if one single log would ever have left the spot where it lay in the heart of the forest.

(Hand-hauling was an operation that was, even then, on the verge of extinction. The very large companies, such as African Timber and Plywood, the giant Unilever subsidiary based in Nigeria and Gold Coast, already had log-hauling crawler tractors operating in many of their areas by the early 1950s.)

Raft construction was an art in itself. Each log, when it arrived at the waterside from the forest, had a timber dog driven into each end to allow the rope which would link it to the others to pass through. Not all species were floaters; indeed, some of the heavier species sank like rocks when they were jacked into the water. This was where those renowned watermen, the Ijaws, came into their own. They supplied most of the expertise in the making of the rafts and their subsequent navigation through the narrow creeks to the shipping point. The heavier logs were rafted by the simple expedient of tying one log between two floaters. Sunken logs would be raised to the surface by the amphibious Ijaws, who would disappear like otters into the dark waters, clutching the end of a length of rope in order to attach it to the sinker. They could stay for ages underwater without coming up for air, grubbing around in the treacly mud at the bottom, with only the steady plop of bubbles on the surface to tell the waiting world that they had not vanished for ever.

The rafts were of long and narrow construction, to allow them easy passage through the narrow channels to the deeper, wider waterways nearer the coast. Contract gangs of Ijaws poled them all the way, sleeping and eating aboard them, oblivious to the incessant attacks of tsetse and horseflies by day and the clouds of mosquitoes by night. They ate fish until they were practically growing scales; they froze when the nightly harmattan mists enveloped them, and they got battered by unseasonal rainstorms. Yet I never saw a rafter that was unhappy, or one that failed to greet you with a big smile and a wave as you passed him by on your motor-boat. These were men who were happy at their work. Like all such men, they more than earned their corn.

My memories of those waterways remain vivid and joyful. They were peaceful, and the sun shone hot and bright over them during the long months of the dry season, an often welcome respite from the eternal gloom of the rainforest. I remember the delicate cedar-fragrance of bruised mahogany bark and the aroma of exotic spices from the village cooking pots. I remember long-legged lily-trotters padding daintily over the vegetation atop the languid waters and the hornbills flapping noisily and in most ungainly fashion among the stilt-rooted trees at the water's edge.

But mostly, I remember the raftsmen, laughing and singing as they roped their logs together, preparing them for the first part of their odyssey to cold and alien lands.

For the most part, though, my work kept me well away from the sharp end of the logging business. Away from human beings, the forest came to life. Colobus monkeys squabbled among the fig trees and the secretive touraco skulked high up in the gallery of the forest. Elephants followed the rivers in the dry season to plunder the fruits of ongokea and ozouga that grew along the banks. Snakes, large and small, were everywhere, from the whip-thin forest cobra to the gross, indolent, utterly lethal gaboon viper. Gaily coloured weavers hung their incredible nests around the swamp verges and wild pigs, lean and agile as whippets, fled snorting through the undergrowth. Occasionally the homicidal buffalo would dispute right of way as you returned to your camp in the evening, and the sudden cough of a prowling leopard would make you huddle just that little bit closer to your camp fire during the long African nights.

The time passed quickly. I trekked far each day through these endless forests, paddled many miles in dug-out canoes, and drank gallons of palm wine with the happy-go-lucky forest people. Each morning I woke to the cheerful song of the pepperbird and this Utopian existence was for ever and ever . . .

I was wandering along the dockside of a sweltering African port when I spotted someone whom I knew to be connected with the timber trade. He was one of a new breed of timber man who had suddenly appeared on the Coast, dynamic and full of modern ideas about how to do things better and faster and, especially, how to make more and more money faster and faster. 'Africa Time' was not for this young man. At this moment he was supervising the loading of a number of wooden crates onto his truck. Noting my obvious interest, he remarked: 'Take a good look at them, Mac, for what is inside those crates is going to change the timber industry here for good!'

Curiosity now fully aroused, I asked him to reveal all.

'These,' he replied smugly, 'are chainsaws.'

Chapter 4
THE MEEK SHALL INHERIT

A cynic with the improbable name of Israel Zangwill once asserted that if you were to scratch the Christian, you would find the pagan – spoiled. Like many another ancient saying, there may be a fair amount of truth in it. However, if you had tried to spout that sort of heresy in certain parts of the land of my childhood, the wrath of a very Calvinist God would surely have been brought down upon your heathen head.

Indeed, anything less like the conventional idea of pagans than a gaggle of matrons heading for their weekly dose of religion in the days of my youth would have been difficult to imagine. Summer and winter, rain or shine, the Sabbath morning would see them wending their way sedately up the road to the wee kirk, dressed in their Sunday best. They were as sombre of garb as the rooks that wrangled in the elm tops, with their sweeping gowns, long silk gloves and darkly veiled hats that served to ensure that every square inch of flesh be covered lest some lustful ploughhand gaze lewdly upon them *en passant*. Half-hidden behind their veils they wore their Sunday faces – expressions of austere devotion that they had begun to practise the moment they had got out of bed in the morning, and which they obviously considered as important a part of their Sunday as the hymn book and the Bible. Even when we children set off down the same road to school the following day, it seemed to us as though the faint but unmistakable smell of mothballs and geraniums still lingered in the morning air about the hedgerows.

Religion was a deadly serious business in the land of John Knox back in those days. Our God was a stern and unyielding one, a God of rebuke and retribution. He was a God totally devoid of humour, and those who were chosen to spread His word on earth did so with a fearsome solemnity that must have pleased Him mightily. Saintly smiles were all that was permitted in the House of God, and these only on the rare occasions on which the minister deigned to crack some melancholy witticism. Laughter within the gloomy aisles of the kirk was as welcome as gunshot.

Children had to be particularly circumspect. It was fatal for a child to be seen having too much fun on a Sabbath Day. Digging for worms in the midden down at the farm was definitely taboo, as was the skinning of rabbits and moles on the kitchen table. Having fun on the Lord's Day was forbidden, particularly where His lambs were concerned. This was a Day of Rest, and God Himself could not have helped you dodge the flak from the 'Unco Guid' if you did anything to disturb the sanctity of His Day.

We were more fortunate than most. Our parents were more understanding and, while our mother maintained a lifelong – if somewhat tenuous – link with the Protestant kirk, my father seemed to feel less drawn to the call. His was the most laid-back of personalities. Only the news that the minister was coming up the garden path on one of his periodic visits could rouse him from his traditional Sunday afternoon torpor in the big armchair by the hearth. Then he would display a degree of athleticism quite unsuspected by those who knew him only as a drinking companion down in the local pub. Although our little cottage had no back door, this would prove no obstacle whatsoever to father. Long before the minister had stepped over the threshold and into the house, the guardian of our home would have exited through the back window like a ferret, and our last view of him would generally be as he vanished over the brow of the hill behind the house, leaving us to our Christian fate as he headed for points unknown.

But traumas such as these were exceptions. Usually, Sunday was much the same as any other day of the week in our household. So long as we did our sinning well away from prying eyes, no one bothered us much. It was a day for 'guddling', when practised little fingers would tease red-speckled trout from the cool, dark waters of the burn that bordered the Crow Wood behind our house. The trout would be charred black over a stick fire by the burn, then eaten, often half-raw, as our ancestors must have done at the dawn of time.

We were little better than pagans ourselves, and if the distant chimes of the church bells ever brought faint stirrings of religious remorse to our savage little souls as we sat among the bracken picking at the bones of our latest victim, I do not remember it now.

The word 'pagan' came to the English-speaking world as a fairly loose interpretation of the late Latin word 'paganus', meaning 'civilian'. Somehow or other, patristic scholars around the 4th century AD managed to dump poor old 'paganus' under the classification of 'heathen', meaning just about anyone not, in their own words, 'a soldier of Christ'.

Soldiers of Christ were pretty heavily outnumbered in the feculent swamps of West Africa when I first went out there, so God alone knows what the first Portuguese thought when they arrived in the Bight of Benin around the middle of the 13th century. They must have reckoned that they were anchored at the very gates of hell. It took another couple of hundred years before anything other than cautious exploration and trading was attempted by them. Then, in perhaps the greatest tour de force in the history of West African theology, those messianic adventurers, the Jesuits, converted the ruler of one of the great coastal tribes, the Jekri, to Christianity.

The old king's hangover on the morning following his enlistment to the cause of Jesus could not have been improved by the knowledge that he had betrayed his tribal gods, but he made the best of a bad show by insisting that he be supplied with a white woman as part of the deal. The resourceful clerics, quite unfazed, paddled off to Sao Tome, a bleak Portuguese possession off the coast of Rio Muni, and brought one right back for him.

What the lady thought of the haute couture and social graces of her new in-laws is not recorded, but she must have proved a suitable consort for the king: to this day, many of the Jekris are of a strikingly light coloration, in marked contrast to the ebony hues of the neighbouring tribes.

Christianity and the dogma of Islam have scythed wide swathes through pagan beliefs nowadays, but there are still, even as I write, those who stick stubbornly to the old ways. Dark forests have always been rife with superstition, and African forests perhaps more so than most. How often have I found in the heart of the rainforests the old familiar offerings suddenly there before me: plaited palm fronds strung head-high over a trail . . . the skull of a monkey perched on a log by a termite mound . . . a dirty white rag hanging limply from a pole at the entrance to a hidden village . . . bowls of food left out at the juncture of an anabranch . . .

Juju is in the very air of Africa and it is deep-rooted in the people of the Coast, from the lowly hunter to the politician. It is to be found wherever one goes and in whatever one does. In one country a cabinet minister known to me was hanged after a lengthy trial in which he was found guilty of dabbling in human sacrifice, while in another the head of a football association with which I was briefly involved said: 'Witchcraft is a sickness that runs throughout the whole of our soccer culture.' There was, in my day, little that was totally free from the pervasive influence of the witch doctor, and it was not unknown for the 'converted' to emerge from their Christian churches in the morning only to begin preparing for the rituals of some pagan festival in the evening. And who could blame them? The converted were simply hedging their bets.

Pagan deities are an absorbing study, if only because of the fact that almost as much blood has been shed in their names as in those of our civilized varieties. Like the Christians, most pagans believe that one deity controls the Universe. It is true that the pagans have plenty of other gods, but they have usually one supremo in charge of the whole works. His title varies from tribe to tribe, but the concept remains the same. He is The Boss. In Nigeria, the Ibos of the east call him Chuku and the Yorubas of the west call him Olorun. In the rainforests of central Africa, the pygmies worship him as Khonvum.

I sat with one of these little people one night by his fire while the god of thunder rumbled all around us and shafts of his eternal fire streaked across the inky sky. It was a night for warlocks to stalk the dark woods and I listened, enthralled, as he related to me how Khonvum made the first pygmies in the sky and lowered them to earth by means of a long rope made of liana. There they found forests full of game, fruit and vegetables, honey and water. Each night Khonvum renewed the sun's energy by collecting fragments of stars in a leather sack and throwing them at the sun. Khonvum, said the little man, is smart enough to leave the general running of earthly affairs to his team of minor gods, but if he has any really important messages to relay to the pygmies, he passes them on through the animals of the forest.

The pygmy listened intently as I told him the story of the Virgin Birth. When I had finished, he spat in the fire. 'Anyone who believes that,' he remarked, 'will believe anything.'

These supreme deities are, generally speaking, benign. They rule mainly by cunning. They are easily satisfied: all they ask of the human race is a lot of praise at fairly regular intervals. They leave the hell-raising to their minions – the lesser gods and spirits who control the destinies of every living thing on earth. Even when they do have a dispute, it is seldom one that degenerates into a vulgar brawl. Conflicts are settled by one trying to prove that he is smarter than the other. A good example of this may be found in Nigerian legend, where Olorun, the sky god, and Olokun, the god of the sea, had a contest to decide who was to be head of the Yoruba pantheon. Thus was the first-ever fashion show born: each was to wear his finest clothes and be judged by the Yoruba people. Olorun left the heavenly catwalk with the sash of honour by the simple expedient of appearing in the guise of a chameleon, thus displaying his superior guile in being able to match instantly anything that his rival might choose to wear.

One of the most important of the Nigerian deities is Ogun. He is the Yoruba war god and, because of his dependency on the skills of blacksmiths and the weapons they produce, he is looked upon as a sort of patron saint of blacksmiths and god of iron.

For one week in each year the towns of Yorubaland reverberate to the sound of drums as troupes of colourfully-garbed musicians and dancers throng their narrow streets during the festival of Ogun. Vehicles are not permitted to pass through towns during the night and may only pass through by day when bedecked with palm fronds. In years gone by strangers have been killed when innocently transgressing this law and I narrowly escaped a similar fate in my early years in Africa. Driving through an apparently deserted town at dead o'night, I came under fire from a veritable fusillade of stones. The fist-sized stones rained down on my Landrover from all quarters, whanging tinnily on the bonnet and roof and sides as I reversed frantically back out of town and into the safety of the surrounding bush.

In the bad old days, Ogun was propitiated by human sacrifice. Things have changed now, at least inasmuch as the casual observer is permitted to know. Many years ago I worked among the beautiful, cool forests of maple-leaved obeche skirting the craggy bluffs of Ondo Province. It was festival time, and I was delighted to be invited to a soiree being held at one of the picturesque little villages scattered around the ancient town of Ondo. Darkness had fallen by the time I arrived and already the huge tropic moon had edged her way up over the black silhouettes of the crags that stood sentinel around us. The night air vibrated to the rhythm of drums and the musical tinkling of tiny 'calabash pianos'. Dancing girls, naked from the waist up, shimmied around in the dust of the compound, their ebony bodies gleaming with perspiration in the silvery, spectral moonlight. Gourds of palm wine and bottles of the traditional illicit 'gin' were much in evidence. The old chief grinned tipsily at me from the shadows. I sat down beside him and accepted the customary offering of gin and kolanut. The gin was raw and evil smelling. The kolanut was dry and bitter as gall.

Much, much later I found myself tucking into a bowl of thin and very peppery stew. It was quite good, though, and I asked the chief what sort of meat it contained. 'Dog,' he said briefly.

Maybe it was, indeed, dog. But to this day I sometimes wonder. I cannot help recalling that he had a wicked glint in his eye as he spoke, and it is a fact that he and a collection of minor chiefs were arrested later that year for the suspected ritual murders of children . . .

There are literally thousands of minor gods and spirits, and many of them are to be found on earth in the form of animals, birds and plants. On the Upper Niger the Bambara venerate the wood spirit Pemba, found in riverine forest as a small tree covered in thorns. The Sapoes of Liberia regard swallows as spirits of happiness. A common feature of any Sapo village is a tall pole stuck in the centre of the compound, thatched with palm fronds and with a ring of thorns halfway up as a barrier against predatory cats and snakes, so that swallows may rest in safety under its umbrella. It is believed that no harm can befall a village in which swallows feel safe to sleep at night.

Water spirits figure prominently in the lore of West Africa. There are numerous legends of water leopards that live in small rivers and streams, lying in wait for women and children as they come to bathe in the evenings. In Cameroon, many claim to have seen Poutch N'Diem, the water stallion. He is reported to be white in colour, with red, black-rimmed eyes, scarlet lips, and a long, multi-coloured mane, a description which could fit rather a lot of the humans of indeterminate sex witnessed by my aged eyes in our larger cities since my return to western civilization.

One of the most widespread of the legends concerns Anansi, the spider god of West Africa. Anansi lives entirely by his wits and he can assume a number of guises. He fears only Gum-Girl. Gum-Girl is in fact a thief-trap, a wooden effigy covered in sticky latex, and she is the brain-child of an irate farmer whose crops are being stolen. Soon after the farmer had placed the effigy at the entrance to his farm, Anansi arrived. Irritated by Gum-Girl's continued silence in response to his overtures, Anansi allowed the male chauvinist in him to take control. He informed Gum-Girl that if she did not pay him the deference that his exalted status deserved, he would kick the living daylights out of her. This threat having failed to produce the desired response, he proceeded to beat her savagely. When the farmer returned some time later, he found Anansi stuck more firmly to Gum-Girl than ever he, Anansi, could have bargained for. The thrashing that the unfortunate Anansi received from the vengeful farmer is mimed with much hilarity in every village on the Coast whenever the Anansi legends are being recreated. The Anansi fables followed the slave trade to the United States of America, where they became immortalised by Joel Chandler Harris in the Uncle Remus stories.

Pagan mythology has not always been the instigator of such happy malarkey. More often than not, tribal tenets are carried from generation to generation on undercurrents of sheer terror – fear of enemies, known and unknown, and of the malignant spirits that haunt the dark corners of the forest by night and by day. Greatest of all, though, is the dread of the secret societies that ply their evil trade along the Coast from Sierra Leone to the Congo. They are all-powerful, and they have a terrible hold over the lives of those in whose domain they fester. They rule entirely by fear, and the stench of blood is never too far from the nostrils wherever they gather to practice their odious rites.

Colonial governments did their best to eradicate the more barbaric practices of the societies. They never managed to stamp them out completely, but they were successful in curbing some of their more public excesses. Mostly, though, the cults – secretive enough before – were simply driven underground. They became even more clandestine in their activities. Fishermen all along the Gulf of Guinea now had to exercise extreme care when the time came to smother new-born babies in the mud of their shores to propitiate their gods. Likewise, deep in the forests of the Ivory Coast the hunters of the little bush elephant had to keep a good lookout while stuffing infants into the bellies of their newly slaughtered prey. Those who flouted the colonial laws soon found out that a Christian death by hanging was just as final as – if less protracted than – death by ritual sacrifice.

Nothing much changed in Liberia. In this quasi-American colony – the self-styled 'Land of the Free' – the secret societies flourished. Unfettered by the irksome restraints imposed by the administrators of French and British territories, the Liberian cults ran riot. Indeed, there were times when they virtually ruled the nation. It is no coincidence that in recent times this country has had to endure a succession of the most corrupt and brutally repressive regimes in the turbulent history of West Africa.

In my time, cannibalism certainly existed on the Coast. It probably still does in remote areas. But wherever it did occur, I never knew it to be anything more than ritual cannibalism. I have met those who claimed to have eaten human flesh, but never as a gastronomic preference. It has never been too hard to find proof of this – the mangrove swamps and sluggish estuaries of the Coast have always provided a handy repository for what was left of cadavers after the societies have finished with them. From time to time along that lonely shoreline, bits and pieces of what had once been human beings would be washed ashore and the same grim rumours would be recycled on the bush telegraph. The cults were back in business.

The Leopard Society was a particular menace. The cool nights of the harmattan at the end of the year would invariably herald a renewal of its activities. Workers on rubber and tea plantations trembled in their huts at night, afraid to venture out for fear of attack. Women living in remote areas were particularly vulnerable when collecting firewood or going down to the river at sunset. The body would be left where it dropped, with deep lacerations on the back and neck to simulate leopard attack. The human involvement was usually evidenced by the fact that the heart would be missing – excised neatly from the body and carried off into the forest for the macabre rituals.

After their annual orgies, the members of this most elusive of all African cults seemed to vanish into thin air. But not always into complete anonymity, for few secrets can remain hidden in the forests of the White Man's Grave. For a time, I had a Leopard Man working for me – not that I was aware of this fact when I employed him. Indeed, I did not become aware of it until after he died.

I had hired him as a humble trace-cutter for my survey gang and the thing most immediately noticeable about him was his heavily cicatriced face, which gave him the appearance of an ornately decorated black pot. The other memorable thing about him was his veritable jaw-breaker of a name – Mgbemezirinnandi Obi.

Apart from his quite startling facial markings, though, he was just about the most nondescript human being I had ever seen in my life. He was little more than pygmy-sized, as thin as a stick-insect, and he had the furtive, brow-beaten air of the archetypal henpecked husband. But he had no wives that I ever heard of, nor – unusually for an African – did he show the slightest desire for the company of either women or men. He was the complete loner, to the extent that even his fellow workers shunned him. Perhaps this alone should have sounded warning bells for me, for the average African is a carefree, gregarious sort of person, not given to long, introspective silences. But he was a reliable worker, going about his allotted tasks quietly and efficiently enough, albeit with a sort of obsequious resignation. When, towards the end of the year, he asked for a couple of weeks off work to return to his homeland far to the east as his father was dying, I readily acquiesced. I never saw him again.

I suppose that he would have faded forever from my memory but for the way in which his life ended. Some months later I was summoned to my headquarters, a sprawling timber port several hundred miles away on the Niger Delta. Awaiting my arrival was an English colonial police officer with whom I was already acquainted and whom I knew to be one of the country's most senior murder investigators. He quizzed me for a time about my erstwhile employee and I gave him what little information I had on the man. In the end, unable to contain my curiosity, I asked him why he should be so interested in such a nonentity. 'Because,' he replied in a matter of fact tone, 'I have just shot him.'

His was an interesting story. A spate of murders on the little farms bordering the Great River had been virtually ignored by the powers that be until the slaying of an eminent black politician's daughter. She had been struck down on her father's cocoa farm as she returned to her hut in the evening with a pan of water on her head. Like the other victims, she had been mutilated, her neck and shoulders ripped open by razor-sharp claws. Her heart had been removed.

The wheels of justice, hitherto so leaden of movement when the victims had been simple peasants, now went into overdrive. Armed police were drafted in from all over the region for surveillance duties. My friend was in charge of them. Sitting on a log by the edge of a plantation one moonlight night with a double-barrelled shotgun cradled on his knee, he saw a shadowy figure emerge from the bush about 15 yards away. He flicked on his torch. Caught in the sudden glare of light, the figure paused, startled, then dived like a rabbit for the cover the trees. Without hesitation, the policeman fired.

Mgbemezirinnandi Obi was stone dead when his executioner reached him, riddled through and through by the heavy buckshot. On his body were the terrible tools of his trade: the leopard skin tied securely around his head and shoulders, the deadly claws of iron strapped to his fingers, and the long, thin-bladed knife for butchering his victims.

Small, obsequious men fill me with disquiet to this day, and the Biblical exhortation that the meek shall inherit the earth no longer has the salutary effect upon me that it used to have.

Christianity did not come easily to the Coast. Indeed, the degree to which the ordinary bush African was prepared to tolerate the various sub-species of religion that civilization attempted to foist upon him, seemed to me to depend greatly on how easy-going and colourful that particular brand of religion happened to be. The grey, flinty inflexibility of the early Protestant evangelists held little attraction for the carefree, highly polygamous African of the bush. Few concessions were made to customs and beliefs that had been part and parcel of his way of life since long before the time of Christ. The pagan was expected to accept, instantly and without equivocation a dogma that was, for the most part, in complete contradistinction to the very essence of his being. The colour, pageantry, gaiety and the drama of pagan worship was to be cast aside – eradicated and forgotten – to be replaced by the forbidding drabness of the Reformist. It was to be Calvin versus the witch doctor and his picturesque fetishes.

Although, in reality, it was a much more profound conflict than that. It was the Calvinist versus the whole of Africa. This head-on confrontation had little hope of winning over the hearts and minds of such happy-go-lucky people, and there was a lofty arrogance in the approach of the zealots that sceptical agnostics such as I found difficult to understand.

While Islam had few real challengers in the grasslands and

deserts of the north, it made little impact south of them. Those tall, elegant nomads of the open savannah, the Fulani, were Muslims through and through, but they had a horror of the dripping shades of the tall trees and their foetid, tsetse-ridden swamps. They made sporadic trips down the long, winding trails to the coastal markets to sell their rangy, hump-backed cattle, but when their cows had gone they did not hang around long in the perpetual haze of the sweltering city. They tucked their money into the folds of their long white gowns and took the first train north to where they could still see the sun and there were fewer things to bite them.

It was left to the disciples of Rome to take up the ecclesiastical cutlass for the soul of the bush African. It proved to be no contest.

The Catholic missionaries adopted an approach that was to pay them handsome dividends. They opted for infiltration rather than confrontation. Tolerance was to be the keyword; tolerance and a genuine desire to get to know as much about this savage land and its people as any white man ever could, about its customs and beliefs and traditions, while at the same time endeavouring to spread the message of their own particular faith. It was to be a benevolent kind of dictatorship.

Many of the missionaries I met on my travels were Irish, rough-hewn old Gaelic footballers from the wet green fields of Cork, Mayo and Galway. They were tough as bog oak, but then the bush African liked his mentors to be tough. Just so long as there was a sense of justice to temper the toughness. And the priests had a ribald, very African sense of fun that observed few racial or social barriers. On more than one occasion, while wandering round some busy village market on a Sunday afternoon, I have been drawn as iron filings to a magnet by screams of laughter from a crowd of black mammies clustered round a rubicund old Father sitting on a stool and spinning them off-colour tales in their own tongue. It was little wonder that market women packed the churches everywhere throughout West Africa when characters like these were performing.

Priest and pagan joined forces in trying to make this new religion one that everyone would find easy to understand. The end results were sometimes a little unusual, to say the least. One remarkable missionary in Nigeria set the great wood carvers of Ekiti to work on constructing mahogany panels with religious motifs for church and hospital doors. He allowed the carvers a fair amount of poetic licence in their interpretation of Biblical events. As a result, the Scriptures took a most unholy pounding from the fun-loving and imaginative Ekitis. Startled visitors to missions throughout the land would find themselves confronted with massive church doors adorned with exquisitely engraved tableaux of Negroid Marys pounding yams for the Last Supper, and Ekiti-featured Wise Men bearing calabashes of palm wine on their heads to celebrate the birth of distinctly Yoruba Jesuses.

But, in the end, what really clinched it for the Catholics was their adoption of pidgin English in their teachings. Pidgin English is the lingua franca of West Africa and a good knowledge of it is a virtual necessity for communication. It is marvellously expressive, and it is spoken wherever one goes on the English-speaking Coast. Completely unrelated tribes, separated not only by geography but by language and culture and centuries of mutual distrust, converse in it when their canoes meet on some God-forsaken creek among the mangroves. Traders all over the Coast conduct their business in pidgin English, and black parliamentarians hurl insults at each other in pidgin across the floor of their respective Houses during their occasional flings with democracy.

The Catholic missionaries even incorporated it into the Bible:

'For six days de Lawd He work an' He done make all t'ing — everyt'ing He done put for Eart'. Plenty Beef, plenty cassava, plenty banana, plenty yam, plenty pepper, plenty groundnut – everyt'ing. An' for de wata He put plenty kinda fish an' for de air He put plenty kinda bird.

'After six day de Lawd He tire small-small an' He done go sleep. An' when He sleep, plenty palaver begin for dis place wey dem de call Hebben. Dis Hebben na de place where we go for lib after we done die if we do better t'ing for dis Eart'. De angeli dem lib for Hebben an' play banjo an' get plenty fine chop an' plenty palm wine.

'De headman for dem angeli, dem call am Gabriel, He dey

when dis palaver start for Hebben. Dere be plenty humbug from one bad angeli, dey call am Lucifer. An' Gabriel he catch Lucifer an' beat am proper an' de palaver he finish one time . . .'

The serpent in the Garden of Eden was the cassava snake and the forbidden fruit, the mango. Adam's fall from grace came, not by way of the apple, but because Eve had added mango to his groundnut stew. Children in the congregation sat holding their ribs in ecstasies of fright as they listened to how 'de Lawd', breathing fire and brimstone in His awful fury, set off on the trail of the rascally Adam, and they laughed until the tears ran down their cheeks as they heard how 'h'Adamu he go for bush one time' to escape His wrath.

It was all so delightfully, evocatively African. King James and his Authorised Version simply could not hope to compete.

Patta-putta-patta-putta-patta-putta-patta-putta . . . The drums beat a monotonous tattoo in the village clearing. Storm lanterns hung from the branches of the palaver tree in the centre of the compound, casting flickering light and ghostly shadow on the sea of black dancers as they swayed, stamped and shuffled around the tree. A colossal mammy called over to where we sat on stools in front of chief's hut: 'Reverent Fadder like to dance?'

I glanced sideways at my companion, wondering what his reaction to the impish invitation would be. A huge grin spread over his face as he pushed his jug of beer away and stood up. The dancing stopped momentarily and a burst of cheering sent a cloud of fruit bats swirling from the oil palms behind the village as the bulky priest joined his partner on the edge of the shifting throng. The drummers resumed their cadence, louder and more vigorously now – PATTA-PATTA-PATTA-PATTA-PATTA-PATTA. I looked on as white priest and black market woman capered round the palaver tree among the revellers, their feet scuffing up the dust in a rapid sort of Charleston action, like demented fowl scratching in the dirt. Every so often, as if on cue, they would whirl around and dance back to back, bumping their ample buttocks against each other in the ritual of the dance, to the immense delight of the crowd. The palaver tree, I could not help but note, was a mango.

There was laughter in the village compound that night, spontaneous and infectious laughter, a very African sort of gaiety. But there was something else there too, something intangible, something beyond the scope of a white man's understanding, a sultry mixture of dark sensuality, throbbing excitement and black mystery that pervaded the hot, still air of night as profoundly as the heady perfume of the moonflowers clinging to the mud wall behind my head.

I leaned back against the wall of the hut and watched as the dust rose slowly over the heads of the dancers into a sky glittering with stars. What would my forefathers, I wondered, have made of this scene? And what did the Great Ones – the white man's God and the black man's multifarious deities – think of it? Did the white man's God really approve of His consecrated priests dancing with black pagans? And what about me? Would my very presence at this pagan festival be enough to banish me forever from the white man's Heaven? Or were they starting to integrate Up There too? Black spirits cohabiting with white angels? Khonvum and Olorun and Chuku sharing their palm wine with God and Jesus and the Virgin Mary?

I was interrupted in my musings by the return of the priest. He was sweating profusely. 'This is harder work that giving Mass,' he said as he sat down beside me and reached for his beer.

Much later that night we sat down at a long plank table to eat. Africans, like their white counterparts at junkets the world over, love to make speeches. Speaker after speaker rose to pay effusive tribute to the deity in whose honour we were gathered. The litanies seemed endless. At last, the master of ceremonies turned his head in our direction. 'Would the Reverend Father care to bless our god of the forest?' he asked diffidently.

From somewhere out there, beyond the black silhouettes of the trees, there came a low rumbling of thunder. A sudden flare of cold green light shimmered eerily in the night sky as the soft brogue of Galway wafted quietly and eloquently across the village compound. Here was a truly Christian priest giving his blessing to a festival as old as time itself.

It seemed a fittingly Irish end to a very African night.

Chapter 5

NOVEMBER CHERRIES

You know that the rains are over when the bush cherries come into season. Slender stems of trees barely three inches in diameter – so insignificant that you never notice them for most of the year as they hide demurely in the shadow of their monumental neighbours – suddenly sprout clusters of berries. Spindly, knobbly sticks of things that were bare only a few short days before are now covered in bunches and bunches of fruit, from ground level up to an arm's length above your head. They don't look a bit like cherries at this time, more like clusters of green frog spawn as they hang, close to the parent stem, in the permanent gloom of the tall trees. They don't look much more like cherries a week or two later, not even when they ripen to a gleaming scarlet hue, ready for eating. But that is what the people of the forest call them. Bush cherries. They love them. You are glad to see them, too, and not just because they are good to eat. You are glad to see them because they are final, irrefutable confirmation that the long, dreary rains are over at last.

Cherry time in November. This is my favourite time in the tropics. For me, it is the equivalent of spring in the temperate zone. There is an excitement in the air, a stirring of life, a freshness and warmth in the sunlit days after the chill and the wet and the numbing ennui of the rains. The storms may still boom over the pygmy forests of central Africa, but here in the coastal forests of the White Man's Grave the skies are suddenly blue and cloudless. And so they will remain until the next time, six months hence.

But they don't call it rainforest for nothing. For six months of the year, from May to October, it rains and it rains and it rains. During the whole of those six long months, Mother Africa hardly ever closes the sluice gates. This is a downpour of such unremitting proportions as can only be properly imagined by those of us who have lived through a West African rain season.

It begins innocuously enough. The first rumbles come from over the sea far to the south, just a faint, low growling sound from somewhere away below the horizon, inaudible to those who live deep in the forest and just barely audible to those who live by the sea. This first time, it doesn't last long. The growling soon subsides to little more than a discontented muttering and fades into nothing with the setting of the sun as the storm takes itself off over the vast, hot wastes of the Gulf of Guinea.

There is usually a lull for a couple of days, then it starts up again. Now, those who live by the coastline will see a darker wash of colour on the horizon and where blue of ocean and sky meet, a narrow, dark-grey band widens almost imperceptibly. It creeps inexorably shorewards over sea and sky, a gunmetal grey that receives fitful illumination from the faint flickerings of the electric storm fretting far out over the water. The growling is back but this time it doesn't go away. This time it becomes progressively louder as the sapphire cloak of the sea is slowly replaced by a mantle of sullen, liquid lead, and the dry, burning orb of the sun is transformed into a harsh, watery glare. There is oppression in the air and a brooding, suffocating heat fills the being with a lowering sense of depression, an unaccountable feeling of doom and foreboding. There is a sense of tense expectancy everywhere, and when the sudden breeze that presages the storm hits the land at last, it is almost with a sense of relief that the people of the Coast settle down to await the arrival of the rains.

The first storms are at their most dramatic in the forest interior. This is particularly so in the vicinity of crags and mountain ranges. Great clattering bursts of thunder shake the earth with their violence, and lightning flares and sears and splits the heavens in a continuous brilliance of cold yellows and greens beyond the dark of the trees.

These first storms bring wind with them too, a wind that flurries and swirls and shrieks through the forest in demoniac rage. Cannonballs wallop together overhead and ricochet around the surrounding hills in a hellish cacophony of noise as all the gods in the firmament hurl everything they can find at each other in their terrible fury while mere mortals cringe in whatever scrap of shelter they can find down in the wild, wet woods.

Those early storms are the ones that cause the real damage in the rainforest. At any time of the year the traveller's sleep may be disturbed by the sound of elderly giants crashing to the ground, but these are only occasional sounds, a natural sorting out of the sick and the dying. But at the beginning of the rains the elements combine their mighty forces to create a special kind of havoc. Great trees are incinerated by lightning bolts and others are uprooted and flung aside by the Brobdingnagian power of the wind, to lie shattered and lifeless in a tangle of liana on the forest floor. Here and there on hillsides and exposed river banks, swathes are blasted through the forest by the tornadoes to form incredible morasses of fallen trees and thorny vines, impenetrable to all but the smallest of creatures.

But the ferocity of those early storms soon fades. As suddenly as they started, they stop. The forest settles down to the humdrum monotony of the rain season proper.

And monotony it certainly is. The air is now still and the rain comes down in a relentless torrent, sheets of it, so heavy that, in the gloom of the great trees, it is often impossible to see more than 10 yards ahead. It seems barely possible that such rain can last for long. But it does, month after month of it, with hardly a pause for breath. It is an emptying of the heavenly bladders on a grand scale, a deluge of truly Noachic proportions.

Only foolishness or hunger makes anyone venture outside during those months. Main roads become little better than ploughed tracks, blocked by abandoned vehicles along their lengths, and rivers become completely impassable, their bridges ripped asunder and whisked away by the irresistible force of the water. Such naked, primitive power is awesome to behold and nothing at all can withstand it. Water levels rise 10 feet overnight and rivers that had been as quiet as English chalk streams one day become roaring torrents the next.

The Owena in Nigeria is one such river. For much of the year it is a placid river and, in places, rather a pretty one. It first sees daylight somewhere among the rocks and elephant grass of the Ekiti savannahs, meandering through the dry obeche forests of northern Ondo, then south through the wet opepe and abura bush of the Binis until it joins the queue of rivers jostling shoulder to shoulder at the confluence of the vast Niger Delta. It is a long journey, but for most of the way it is a gentle procession, with such a musical tumbling of cool clear waters over gravel beds that one might be forgiven for expecting to see salmon rising to the fly in the eddies behind the larger boulders.

But there is nothing placid about it in the rains. Then, it is transformed into a thundering, rolling brown flood that stops for nothing. Everything in its path is uprooted and taken with it in its mad charge for the Bight of Benin.

Here and there along its course bridges had been built over it sometime after the end of World War II. These were mainly the work of the concessionaire who owned the timber rights in the surrounding forests. They were of very solid construction indeed. They had to be. A terrific volume of traffic hurtled over them daily at breakneck speed, mostly articulated lorries piled high with massive logs. There was a standard design for this type of bridge: abutments and piers were monoliths of stone and concrete, each pier being 15 feet long by five feet wide and tall enough to ensure clearance above the river at its optimum rain season height. For double security, each of those piers was bolted into the bedrock of the river. Spanning the piers were great baulks of ironwood, three feet square, and, secured to the tops of those beams with six-inch nails, the heavy plank decking and running strips required for the bridge surface.

Looking at them, one would have been convinced that nothing the elements could hurl at them would have been capable of inflicting the slightest damage to them. That, certainly, is what I thought until the rain season of 1957.

That season produced the heaviest rains seen for many decades on the Coast. I was working in the forests of the northern reaches of the Owena and the end of one particular day found me in a Land-Rover churning its way south through seas of mud to our first bridge crossing. We reached it and stopped, thunder-struck. The river, admittedly heavily swollen when we had crossed it four hours earlier, had risen a further eight feet and was now rolling on its merry, muddy way over the topmost planks of the bridge surface. One hundred feet of the bridge surface was quite invisible to us, hidden as it was by the chocolate-brown spate waters. Stuck behind the bridge was the most incredible assortment of debris one could have possibly imagined: log ends, tree limbs, great piles of bushes festooned with liana, pitsawn planks, an upturned canoe, even one massive okwen tree which had been torn out by its roots further upstream and was now jammed firmly behind one of the piers. An umbrella of its huge branches hung high over the bridge, and wedged in droll abandonment atop them was the body of a drowned cow.

The whole bridge structure shook and shuddered and groaned before the pressure of it all, and what had looked so rock-solid to my eyes earlier that day, now looked decidedly less so. I would happily have gone straight back up the road and lodged in the timber camp with the workers for the night – indeed, had I been older and wiser, I should certainly have done so – but my driver, Michael, was made of sterner stuff. He was not for turning. Besides, I happened to know that he had a greater incentive for wishing to cross the river than I. A new and exceedingly pretty girlfriend awaited him in his little village 40 miles to the south of this bridge, and he had every intention of reaching her this very night. While he had much confidence in her integrity, he had no confidence whatsoever in his predatory bachelor friends should he be forced to spend a night or two away from her. So he put the vehicle into gear and moved slowly towards the river, while I sat in the passenger seat and did what all pagans do in times of extreme danger – I prayed to God that I'd be good forever and ever if He could only see His way to getting me safely over this damned bridge.

Crossing that bridge was one of the few genuinely foolhardy things I have ever done in my life. Most of the decking was already under a two-feet deep, fast-flowing torrent of brown water, and it was impossible to see whether the bridge still, in fact, existed at all under it. All that the driver could do, therefore, was to keep his gaze riveted on the point of the opposite bank at which he could just discern the top of the bridge abutment rising above the water, and drive straight towards it. With heart-stopping slowness, he did just that, the bridge shuddering violently under our wheels and the roof of the vehicle scraping through the overhanging branches of the okwen and under the belly of the cow as we edged our way towards the distant shore.

Several lifespans later a collection of naked urchins standing in the bucketing rain watching our progress raised a cheer as we pulled up alongside them on the far bank. Michael switched off the engine and lit a cigarette with shaking fingers. I stopped praying.

We watched for ten minutes while the waters rose higher and the shuddering death groans of the bridge increased in volume. Finally, with one almighty, scrunching crack, it was gone. Two great concrete piers went tumbling end over end downstream and ironwood beams weighing several tons each were swept off like matchsticks. The planks and beams held together by those six-inch nails were pulled apart as easily as one might pull a cocktail stick from a sliver of cheese. The mighty okwen tree took off at a rate of knots on the bosom of the floodwaters, heading the procession of flotsam with the cow's body still straddling the branches like some obese surf-rider charging for shore on the crest of a Hawaiian wave. The bizarre cortege swept regally round a bend on the river, to vanish from our ken forever.

If one had to travel at all in the rain season, it was better to do so on foot. At least, that was my belief. Even the best and most powerful of vehicles could get bogged down inextricably, an intimidating prospect when far from home in lands where the benisons of automobile associations were unheard of. The traveller on foot had only himself and his few possessions to worry about. Stranded vehicles were sitting ducks for enterprising collectors of vehicle parts, of which there was always a surprising number even in the more remote and unlikely localities. Engines would be removed in short order, and many's the tale of woe I have had from drivers who awoke in the morning after a night's rest in their cars to find that it was now sitting on blocks, all the wheels having vanished during the hours of darkness.

I never had those problems. For much of time my legs were my transport and the forest was my home. My life was governed by what was known as 'Africa Time'. If circumstance decreed that it was impossible for me to get from A to B today, well, there was always tomorrow. If a river proved impassable and there was no canoe to ferry me across, what of it? The obvious solution was to wait until the waters subsided. Tomorrow. The next day. Next week. Whenever. What was the hurry, anyway? Living and working with the people of the forest, one developed the patience of the grey heron and the philosophy of mañana.

It was a necessary philosophy in the rain season. The whole forest just had to hunker down and stick it out. Stoicism became an art form here. The few creatures that actually liked the rain were seen more frequently and those that didn't, ventured out only when necessity drove them out. Man was encountered but rarely, and then usually in the form of the occasional hunter looking for something to fill the bellies of his wives and children.

I was no more fond of the rains than the next man but I got used to them. I had to. My work in cataloguing tree species went on throughout the year, rain or shine. I never made the slightest attempt to stay dry when out working, and indeed in well over a quarter-of-a-century of work in the forests of the White Man's Grave I never once carried waterproof clothing with me. It would, in any case, have been a waste of time; too hot and cumbersome for the amount of walking I had to do, and the condensation inside coat and leggings would have nullified the whole point of the exercise. Rubber boots, too, were worse than useless – they simply filled with mud and water at the first swamp crossing. My policy was to keep it simple: the lightest possible clothing, and lightweight boots with canvas uppers and rubber soles, similar to those worn by basketball players, which would be purchased at any market stall in West Africa for just a few dollars. So clad, you realised that you were going to get wet the moment you stepped out into the rain, but at least your movements were less restricted than if you were wearing rain gear. In any case, once you got used to the morning chill of the rain, you were as comfortable as anyone could ever hope to be who had to work outside in the rain season.

There were some advantages to working in the rain. For one thing, one got closer to the wildlife. Sometimes, too close. The relentless downpour seemed to have the same brain-deadening effect on wild creatures that it had on human beings. Trudging along a forest path with my eyes on the ground and the rain battering me, I have found myself – to our mutual discombobulation – in the midst of herds of bush pig and giant forest hog. The number of close encounters I have had with the mentally unstable forest buffalo does not bear thinking about. Once when I was on the edge of a clearing of young umbrella trees a herd of elephants stampeded all around me, flattening everything in their flight, and I have all but shaken hands with families of chimpanzees in the great, wet forests bordering the Mano River on the Sierra Leone boundary.

But it is some of the less obvious inhabitants of the forest that claim the attention most in the rain season. Now is the time for *Bitis nasicornis* to go on patrol. This is the rhinoceros viper, so called by scientists because of the warty horns on his snout. Because of his love of the rain and watery places he is known as the River Jack to the forest people. To the impartial observer he is extraordinarily beautiful, patterned as he is in such a striking array of reds, yellows, greens, blues and blacks. But you must keep a sharp lookout when in his kingdom; despite his remarkable coloration, he is surprisingly difficult to see on the forest floor. Unlike his more placid cousin the gaboon viper, he has a filthy temper, but, just like the gaboon viper, his strike is absolutely lethal.

The earthworm goes on tour at this time of the year, too, But this is no ordinary earthworm. This is an earthworm the likes of which you have never seen before in your life. This is the African earthworm, the grandaddy of all earthworms. The first time I ever saw this perfectly harmless invertebrate writhing down the path towards me, all six slimy feet of it and one inch thick from beginning to end, I experienced a thrill of horror such as I had never experienced before and have never experienced since. I stepped aside and watched it as it humped its way blindly past me, silent as a ghost and moving determinedly down the thin runnel of water which flowed along the centre of the path. With surprising speed and agility it disappeared round the bend, going, I suppose, nowhere in particular, but going there with the fixity of purpose that might have been exhibited by some elderly tippler heading for his favourite pub at opening time.

As might be expected, swamp life comes into its own during the rains. Waters that have stagnated during the dry season become revitalized and spawn a new generation of life. Stirring in the murky depths will be the lungfish. This curious and unprepossessing eel-like creature, which can grow to about five feet in length, hibernates for the duration of the dry season in a nest of mud deep down in the swamp. Should the swamp dry out and the mud harden like concrete, this will present no problem for the lungfish. Indeed, it will present no problem to this resilient fish should it have to remain in this same mud coffin for the next four years. Nature has prepared if for just such a contingency. It has gills like any other fish, but it also has lungs for breathing. Curled up snugly in its cocoon of dried mucus and with an air vent near its mouth, this remarkable amphibian just waits for the water level to rise again, living on its fat reserves in the interim, the ultimate example of 'Africa Time' in action. When the water eventually rises and softens the mud enough to enable it to burrow its way back out, it returns to its beat in the waters of the swamp, to the general discomfiture of the frogs and freshwater crabs on which it feeds.

The swamps are also the domain of the marsh mongoose and the clawless otter. Here, too, one will find the pretty sitatunga deer and the water chevrotain. The hunchbacked chevrotain, not much bigger than the European rabbit, looks to the layman like a midget deer. Not so – perhaps predictably – to the scientist. He classifies it with the camel and the pig. It and the very much larger sitatunga are completely at home in the swamps and both will instantly head for water to avoid capture, diving deep under the surface and remaining there until the danger is over.

Swamps are the breeding ground of the malarial mosquito. The onset of the rains sees a rise in the level of the swamps and a consequent increase in the mosquito population. No insect anywhere is considered a greater health hazard. Oddly enough, the male – recognizable by his feathery antennae – is a completely harmless nectar drinker. It is the female of the species that does the damage, to misquote that arch-chauvinist Rudyard Kipling. West African mosquitoes can shove their needles through denim, and, in addition to transmitting three different types of malaria, they carry such fatal diseases as yellow fever and elephantiasis.

No one has ever travelled through the African rainforest without having come into contact with the driver ant at one time or another. The first hint of thunder in the air coincides with the start of mass movements over the forest floor by those voracious creatures. They are universally feared and every able-bodied thing moves out of their path right quickly. Anything that won't or cannot is in serious trouble. Driver ants figure prominently in the folklore of the Coast, one popular belief being that the python, before swallowing its victim, will always travel in a wide circle around it to ensure that the dreaded driver ants are not in the vicinity and liable to come upon it as it lies comatose after its meal.

Like all ants, the drivers are organized into workers, soldiers, males and queens. They move in columns, and these columns are flanked by soldiers. The soldiers are formidable warriors: they are jet-black, about an inch long, and they have fearsome pincers on their jaws. Millions of them go on the march at any one time, generally in seemingly endless columns of little more than a few inches wide. Excessively heavy rain seems to disorientate them, however, scattering them all over the place in the surrounding bush, and the unwary traveller may suddenly find himself in a seething mass of them with no apparent means of escape. In such a contingency the answer is to run like hell with a high-stepping gait like a trotting horse, stamping the feet hard on the ground as you go to prevent them from getting a purchase.

Among some tribes driver ants are actually regarded as a blessing. They are the finest pest-control agency in all of Africa. Huts are simply abandoned until the ant hordes have passed through, by which time not a single rat, lizard, cockroach or flea remains. Nothing escapes their attentions. On the downside, there are plenty of horror stories about tethered goats, cows in labour, even injured elephants, being reduced to skeletons in short order. I have myself witnessed the aftermath of a driver ant migration on many occasions. Nothing but bones and feathers remain. Their bite is ferocious, and any unfortunate unable to escape is simply eaten alive. I have often had them attach themselves to me and their tenacity is such that, even when you pull them off you, the body comes away from the head, with the result that their pincers remain buried deep in your flesh.

They are particularly active at night, and they are a horrible nuisance to those who have to sleep in the forest during the rains. There is no really effective way of deterring them, and moving camp in the middle of the night in bucketing rain with everything in the vicinity a seething mass of ants is not for the faint of heart. At such times you think longingly of other lands, and you wonder – not for the first time – what you are doing on this savage continent, where nothing ever comes in moderation.

There are very occasional lulls in the downpour and these are the times that you remember with the greatest pleasure throughout the whole of the rains. They are the times when you waken one morning to the sound of chimpanzees somewhere in the near distance hooting and screaming their delight as a hazy sun breaks through the clouds and the mist drifts slowly through the branches of the forest giants like puffs of silvery cotton candy. They are the times when you are drifting off to sleep and you glimpse the moon peeking demurely down upon you from behind dark and torn clouds, and there is even the occasional day when it stops for a few hours and the waters of the swamp, so unpleasant when you had to wade through them the day before, now look as though they are strewn with rose petals as the rays of the setting sun dance gently over the surface towards you.

But these are rare interludes, soon to become a distant memory as the rain comes down again. Once again, you edge your way over rotting tree trunks spanning raging rivers; once again you flounder through endless swamps. Even when you reach relatively solid ground there is only the drumming of the rain in your ears as you squelch your way through the sodden forest. You are convinced that you will never be dry again and that this time, the rains are going to last forever . . .

And suddenly, as abruptly as it started, it is over. Once again the thunder rattles and clatters over the forests and lightning sears through the leaden clouds. But now there is a difference. Now, there is a subtle change in the atmosphere. The storms drift back whence they originated, back to the mangrove swamps of the coastal lagoons. For a few days they bluster and bellow, for a few days they rage impotently up and down, but every single inhabitant of the Coast knows that this is the end. In a short time the gods of the elements will have packed their bags and taken themselves off over the grey Atlantic to pester someone else and the skies will once again be blue and cloudless as the dry season returns to the Coast.

Mesobotrya barteri, the scientists call it, this slender, knobbly, insignificant little bush skulking under its monumental neighbours in the gloom of the rainforest. God knows what the chimps call it, but they love its fruit. So do I, and I have my own name for them. November cherries.

The emergent sun will bring new life to the wetness of the woods. For the next few months the treetops will ring to the songs of the birds and the chattering of monkeys, and the forest will become, once more, a paradise of perfume and colour. The cherries are the harbingers of this resurgence of life.

Mesobotrya barteri. Botanists have no soul. No one who has ever thought of the significance of this tiny fruit, who has ever pulled bunches of them from the parent stem to quench his thirst at the end of a long, hard trek, who has ever tasted the luscious bitter-sweet tang of them, would ever dream of saddling them for evermore with such a dry, unpronounceable, pedestrian name.

To me, they will always be November cherries. I can taste them even as I write this, and no fruit I have ever had since those days has tasted half as good.

Chapter 6
THE ORIGINAL NATIVE

There are few who return from a lengthy stay in the tropics without some horror story about snakes with which to enthral their friends, be it the colonial wife who has happened upon a perfectly harmless six-feet-long rat snake curled up peacefully in the cot beside the little heir to the family fortunes, or the planter who has been accosted by an irritable cobra while obeying a call of nature. I am no exception. My snake stories have long since banned me from every dinner table in the land. The forests of the White Man's Grave abound with snakes of all shapes and sizes and colours and I think I have encountered most of them in my travels.

There are, I believe, eccentrics who are able to bestow upon reptiles a degree of affection that they seldom, if ever, lavish upon their wives, and who have been known to keep the most lethal of reptiles within the confines of their homes. I am not of their ilk. There are few things about serpents that appeal to me. It is not that I am particularly afraid of them, but I am, in all honesty, rather wary of them, and the degree of my wariness is in direct proportion to the size and deadliness of the reptile in question. But, big or small, venomous or harmless, I rarely seek their company. When I have good reason to suspect that somewhere on the trail in front of me lies one in wait, I endeavour, wherever possible, to give it a wide berth. Fortunately, most creatures of the wild, including snakes, have little desire for contact with human beings themselves, and they will instantly disappear upon the approach of man.

It is just as well, for there is no particular reason why snakes –

especially venomous ones – should afford us this degree of deference. Their defence mechanism is of such sophisticated and horrifying effectiveness as to make them the most feared of all the earth's creatures. Snakes have been sending shivers up and down our collective spines since time immemorial. The very thought of their bite so terrifies us that, even if their venom doesn't kill us, there is a very good chance that the shock of being bitten by them will do the trick.

They have, in addition, more right to be here than we have, for they have been around a good deal longer than we – about a hundred million years longer, as near as dammit. Neither fire nor flood nor ice age could wipe out the snake family, and at time of writing they look perfectly capable of surviving a few more ice ages, not to mention the tenure of man on this earth. They, and the cockroaches, are the supreme survivors.

The majority of snakes are to be found in the warmer parts of the world. In West Africa alone there are about a hundred different species, and a high proportion of those dwell in the humid forests of the interior. Not all of these, thank God, are poisonous, but a few claim the distinction of being listed among the most venomous in the world.

Not surprisingly, snake worship features strongly in the mythology of West Africa and there are snake cults everywhere. Pythons in particular are revered by the fishermen of the Coast, presumably because of these reptiles' fondness for swampy conditions and also on account of the enormous lengths to which they grow. For some tribes, the python is the goddess of fertility, for others it is the god of war, the god of hunting, the god of all water, and so on. To those simple tribes whose thoughts are concentrated more on the belly than on theogony, the python is a gourmet's delight and it is trapped and shot and eaten wherever they find it.

The python is by far the longest of all West African snakes; indeed, one monster caught by a fisherman in an underwater trap was later tape-measured by me at 24 feet and five inches. It is not, however, a poisonous snake, but it is a constrictor, killing its prey by wrapping its coils around it and suffocating it. Although the larger members of this species are obviously quite capable of killing and swallowing human beings, and stories are rife throughout the Coast of them doing so, I have never personally known this to happen. But I, for one, should not care to take a chance on it. Despite a life style in which far too much of my time seemed to be spent up to the waist in ooze, I endeavoured never to be in the position of having to wade through swamps at night, the time when these reptiles are at their most active in search of prey.

For my money, though, the most frightful snakes in the whole of the rainforest are the cobras and the aptly-named giant vipers. They are quite dissimilar in every way and are separated scientifically into two different groups. Cobras are long, thin and agile. They can reach a length of six or seven feet and I have, on occasion, encountered cobras a good deal longer than that. Only two types of this extremely venomous reptile are to be commonly found in the vicinity of the rainforest – the black cobra and the spitting cobra. While both do much of their hunting on the ground, they are adept at climbing trees in search of young birds and eggs, and they are both expert swimmers.

All cobras have short, needle-sharp fangs which they do not hesitate to use when trodden on or cornered. Their venom is contained in glands situated on each side of the head and is squeezed out by powerful jaw muscles through venom canals in the fangs into the victim. The venom of cobras, though small in volume compared to that of the vipers, is very potent indeed. Death can occur rapidly when, as is so often the case, the victim is far from hospital or any form of effective treatment. The venom acts on the nervous system, particularly on heart action and breathing. When death does occur, it is generally due to heart failure.

Possibly the most curious snake in the world belongs to this group, and it is one that was abundant in the Africa of my youth. This is the spitting cobra, or *Naga nigricollis*, to give its walking-out name. This remarkable reptile – slate-grey to black in colour, with a vivid salmon-pink to dark-red throat – is unique in that it has the poison apertures at the front of its fangs, rather than at the tip of them as in other snakes. Thus, while it can employ its fangs in the normal way by striking and simultaneously injecting its venom into the bloodstream of its prey, it can also use them to spray twin jets of venom into the face of a potential foe. This is a purely defensive reaction, but it is a very effective one. When the spray of poison hits the eyes, it causes excruciating pain and, if not rapidly treated, can cause permanent blindness. The cobra's venom is also much more potent than that of most other venomous snakes and, as it can be quite aggressive during the breeding season, this fast and active reptile is one to be avoided at all costs.

It is not only as adults that spitting cobras are aggressive – they can be truculent from the moment they leave the egg. One wee chappie, little more than eight inches long, entered an office in which I was working on my own one quiet Sunday morning. As soon as it saw me, it hissed angrily, inflated its tiny hood, and came straight for me. I despatched it with a well-aimed ink bottle.

They are remarkably accurate when 'spitting' their venom. I was watching a worker sorting out a pile of planks in a timber yard one day when he flushed a small cobra of perhaps two feet in length from the bottom of the stack. Without hesitation, it spat at him. On this occasions, I was lucky enough to be in such a position as to be able to see the spray of clear venom glittering in the sun as it sped to its target. This time, the intended victim was lucky; the charge struck him harmlessly on the chin and mouth, just missing his eyes. A rough calculation by me afterwards indicated that this small cobra had been able to direct its jet of venom a distance of some seven feet. It is reasonable to assume that a full-grown cobra would be devastatingly accurate at a much greater range.

There is a theory that the cobra instinctively aims at the face when 'spitting' because sunlight reflects from the eyes and they are thus the brightest part of the body. There may be some truth in this, as old-time zoo collectors generally wore dark glasses or, alternatively, some shining object such as a silver belt buckle on their waists to divert the venom spray when seeking this bad-tempered reptile in awkward situations.

In the absence of proper medicinal eyewashes, bathing the

affected part with milk or water is the normal procedure when one's eyes have been on the receiving end of a spitting cobra's attentions. There are other, less orthodox, methods. I was watching my survey crew at work clearing some scrub in the middle of the forest one hot day at the beginning of the rain season. Standing by my side was an old black hunting friend. As we chatted together, a large cobra reared high up out of the undergrowth directly in front of the labourer next to us and spat right in his face. The lad dropped his machete and staggered back, screaming with pain and clapping both hands over his eyes. My companion sprang into action instantly, hurling instructions at the other workers. With one accord they pounced on the victim, throwing him to the ground and holding him there while the old hunter knelt by his head and urinated in his eyes.

I am not too familiar with the remedial properties of black man's pee, but the treatment certainly worked in this case. When I called to see the victim later that evening, he was sitting in front of his hut drinking palm wine and singing ribald songs with the best of them, little the worse for his experience.

My own career was almost cut short before it had really begun by a spitting cobra. I was walking through thick grass along a boundary line that ran between a forest reserve of towering obeche trees on the one hand, and a cocoa plantation on the other. My companions were a black youth of some 12 years of age and an ancient headman, Gabriel Olaniyen. Progress was slow, as old Gabriel's arthritis was playing up. But I was in no particular hurry; the weather was beautiful and Africa was still very new to me. I had the brashness of the greenhorn about me too, and I had ignored the old man's advice to allow the lad with the machete to walk in front of us in case we encountered any unpleasantness on the way, electing instead to take the lead like the true pioneering warrior that I was.

I was soon to learn my first lesson in survival in the depths of the African bush.

We had walked about 10 miles along the boundary when a sudden explosive hiss from the dense grass around my legs sent a shaft of fear and undiluted horror through me. In the same split second I felt something rolling under the soft rubber sole of my boot, something that felt like a rather thick bicycle tyre, but a tyre that was very much alive and very, very mobile. The thought 'snake' flashed through my mind and I sprang in the air like a gazelle. As I did so, the brute shot out of the grass like a black jack-in-the-box and slashed viciously at me, missing my leg by the merest fraction. For the next 30 seconds – 30 of the longest seconds I shall ever experience in my life – everything was a whirling turmoil of movement as I sprang this way and that in my frantic efforts to avoid the infuriated serpent's fangs. Avoid them I did too, but only God Himself knows how as seven feet of maddened cobra thrashed around my legs while I performed a manic Highland Fling among its coils.

Finally extricating myself somehow or other, I took off up the boundary, moving faster than I had ever moved in my life, intent upon putting as much distance as possible between myself and this hellish thing before my heart and lungs exploded. I suppose I must have covered about 50 yards when I stumbled and fell to the ground, twisting myself round as I collapsed in time to see my *bête noire* some 20 yards behind me and – oh, blessed sight! – turning off into the trees, long black body raised high above the grass and pink hood obscenely extended.

Of my trusty companions, only the boy with the machete was anywhere in sight. He had prudently ensconced himself 40 feet up a palm tree on the edge of the cocoa plantation, from which vantage point he had had a grandstand view of all the action. Old Gabriel, arthritis miraculously cured, had vanished like ectoplasm into the gloom of the forest.

The giant vipers are different in almost every possible way from the cobras. While the cobra is thin, active and aggressive, the viper is fat, sluggish and placid. The cobra lays eggs, while the viper produces large numbers of living young. The cobra's fangs are short and erect, while the viper's fangs are very long and hinged, so that they lie along the roof of its mouth when they are not in use. Also, the viper's venom works in a way that is completely different to that of the cobra. Both are deadly, but for sheer killing potential the giant vipers are, to my mind, the most gruesome exterminators in the whole of Africa.

The giant viper most frequently encountered by me was the gaboon viper; a very heavy snake, even though it rarely exceeds six feet in length. It is hugely fat in proportion to its length a six-foot long specimen could weigh in the region of 25 pounds. It is most strikingly patterned. An indescribable array of geometric triangles, squares and rectangles are etched along the length of its back and sides, in a bewildering mixture of violet, olive, buff and chocolate pastels. Despite its quite startling coloration, it blends uncannily into its background, whether it happens to be lying on the dark floor of the forest or among the brown leaves of a cocoa farm. This, combined with its habitual laziness and its disinclination to move from one's path, makes it a distinct hazard for the unwary traveller.

Fortunately, its very sluggishness sometimes makes it too idle to strike even when trodden upon, and on more than one occasion only its loud, blood-curdling hiss, like air being violently expelled from a gigantic tyre, saved me from the probability of a most unpleasant death.

The gaboon viper's fangs are hollow and resemble curved hypodermic syringes. They are very long − a skull I found many years ago in Sapoba, Nigeria, had fangs measuring two inches. It has a very large volume of venom compared to the cobra, but its venom is less concentrated. Nevertheless, the enormous quantity it injects, combined with the power of its strike and the depth to which it buries its fangs in its victim, can make treatment very difficult indeed.

The chief effect of the gaboon viper's poison is to destroy the blood cells and body tissues. This causes severe internal bleeding and does more than merely kill − the instant breakdown of tissues and blood cells is designed to assist the snake in digesting its prey. (A further complication is that the venom of the gaboon viper is unique in that it contains some of the neuro-toxic characteristics of cobra venom.)

A human being falling foul of one of those awful reptiles far from proper medical treatment is in very serious trouble indeed. His body will be literally eaten away before his eyes by the destructive effects of the venom. Even with immediate treatment, it may take many months for the victim to recover, if ever.

The terrible aftermath of a strike by one of those giant vipers was graphically illustrated to me by an incident in the West African interior. I was standing on the verge of a deserted airstrip awaiting the arrival of a little charter plane which was picking me up for a reconnaissance over a nearby patch of forest, when my attention was drawn to a hullabaloo from the savannah scrub behind me. A few minutes later a small party of Africans trotted out of the elephant grass, bearing on their shoulders a crude litter on which there lay a body. When they spotted me they hurried over and laid the litter on the ground before me.

The elderly white man was in a bad way. He was barely conscious and his face was contorted in agony. He was wearing shorts and his leg was a deep blue-black in colour and dreadfully swollen. The bearers told me that he was an old gold prospector who lived in a shack nearby with his African wife and innumerable children. He had been out shooting partridges in the savannah behind the airstrip when he had trodden on a large gaboon viper. Without hesitation, it had struck him on the knee.

This was long before the days when antivenin became more freely available to we whose lives revolved around the bush. In any case, most of us in those days gave as little thought to the possibility of being bitten by a snake as did, I suppose, the Battle of Britain pilots to the possibility of their being shot down. It always happened to others, but never to oneself. I had no medicaments of any kind, and I hadn't a clue what to do about the old man except listen to his groans.

My plane came in and we carried him onto it. The nearest large hospital was a couple of hundred miles away and he was unconscious long before we got there. But the pilot had radioed ahead for medical help and they were waiting for us at the airport.

He must have been a tough old bird. It took him several months to die. Nevertheless, die he eventually did after a nightmare of prolonged and appalling agony. He needed constant treatment for the massive ulcers that kept erupting all over his body, and constant blood transfusions to counteract the effects of haemorrhaging. His death must have been almost as great a relief to the doctors and nurses attending him as it would have been to the old man himself.

Bitis *gabonica* is its fancy name. The Africans call it the cassava snake. We call it the gaboon viper. Take your pick. But, whatever you call it, you would do well to tread warily when in its territory. Even the mad 'bush cow' in the secret depths of the forest flees when she hears that chilling, explosive hiss of warning about her feet. And where the bush cow fears to tread, then, take it from me, that is no place for we lesser mortals.

Some African legends have it that the serpent in the Garden of Eden was the cassava snake. I should not be all that surprised. Nor would it surprise me greatly if the only thing to emerge unscathed from Armageddon just happened to be that serpent of such sinister beauty, that lethargic and frightful denizen of the White Man's Grave, that was already old when man's time on earth was but beginning.

Chapter 7
THE COLONEL'S LADY

This, we are being constantly assured by the media, is the Era of Girl Power. It is also, they claim, the Age of Equal Opportunity. As the 20th century draws to a close those whose roles in the past were restricted to the bearing and rearing of our children, keeping the home clean and feeding its occupants, now clamour with even more strident voice for the right to equality in everything, including, presumably the right to be considered for employment in such hitherto male domains as municipal rubbish collection, sewer maintenance and slaughterhouse gutting. Perhaps, though, less so for the latter three. These occupations have ever, alas, been lacking in those ingredients vital to the agenda of any self-respecting whiz-kid, male or female: glamour, tons of money, and optimum media exposure.

Television exposure, particularly, is the Sangraal at which they aim. Things have never looked better in this field for the aspirant to Girl Power. Increasingly, it would appear that the criteria for success in television today are that the presenters should be female, very young, slender, and – preferably – blonde. Former masculine bastions such as rugby football, soccer, cricket and – even – boxing reportage have long since succumbed to this heady type of coverage. Even the creatures of the African wild have been engulfed by the relentless march of this sort of Girl Power. We have all seen examples of it at one time or another. Who is there among us who has never been captivated by some television documentary depicting a young lady shooting off reel after reel of film from the safety of her vehicle in order to record at very close range and in distressingly explicit detail, graphic action from the more intimate moments of the love life of the African black rhinoceros?

It is all very educational, no doubt, but one cannot help but feel that one could do with a little more of the old-world chivalry here and a little less of this new-world brashness and desire to know absolutely everything that goes on in the world of nature. Is it much wonder, one is tempted to ask, that the poor beasties always look so sheepish when their act of procreation is over? What, one further muses, would be the bimbo's reaction if she was asked to perform out there in the veldt while the rhino did the filming?

After all the repressions of the past, one is, of course, only too ready to applaud this new mood of self-assertion on the parts of our loved ones. It is long overdue. They have, however, got it wrong in one thing: Girl Power is not new at all. Girl Power has been with us for rather a long time.

It may not have actually started in the White Man's Grave, but Girl Power as exemplified by the wife of the colonial master was a very potent force. She had, of course, a rather different way of expressing it — one could not, for example, imagine the wife of the Governor General as the lead singer with one of our modern pop groups — but everyone, from the lowliest garden boy to the most senior cook, knew who was really in charge in the white man's home. Her husband may have been the official breadwinner, but the power behind the throne was the memsahib.

She was, invariably, as tough as old boots. She had to be, especially the wife who ventured out to the Coast in the early years of the 20th century. The whole environment was against her. From the very beginning, she was fighting Africa: the snakes, the insects, the malarial bouts. It was a never-ending struggle. Disease was rampant. Clouds of bluebottles swarmed on a daily basis to her kitchen from the open latrines around the boys' quarters and the surrounding bush, so that she had to supervise the meticulous washing of every single item of food before it was cooked. Amoebic dysentery was endemic, as was sandfly fever, which resulted in ulceration of the skin and rotting of the liver and spleen. During the day her smaller children had to be protected by mosquito netting while they were resting; not only were there tsetse flies in abundance, but the tombo fly was particularly attracted to sleeping infants. This large fly – something like the European horse-fly – would lay its eggs inside the skin of their heads and necks, eggs which, as they hatched, produced huge boil-like swellings. When these were squeezed, large, fat, gruesomely wriggling white maggots would erupt from them.

The nights provided little comfort for her, either. Often, they were worse than the days. The dripping, mouldering heat of the day seemed to close in on her with a more suffocating intensity within the confines of the mosquito net, her sweat making the sheets soggier by the minute as she tossed and twisted every which way on her bed, unable to bear either the thought of bedclothes on top of her or the heat from the body of her husband snoring beside her.

'In the real dark night of the soul, it is always three o'clock in the morning,' wrote Scott Fitzgerald. There were many such moments for the colonial wife but she made the best of a trying situation, projecting her mind to a Nirvanic future when she and her husband would eventually leave this benighted land to retire to the cool and civilized freshness that was dear old England.

So she stayed. She stayed and she fought and she ruled. She controlled the home, the garden, the compound, her husband's welfare, their social diaries and their personal finances. She was the one who looked after their children, who decided when the time was ripe for the children to return to England for good, and she it was who had the final say on where their children should be educated.

She did no physical labour herself, of course. She didn't have to. She had a small army of servants at her beck and call, and she reckoned that supervising them and trying to cobble together some degree of order out of their daily sloth and inefficiency was quite exhausting enough without having to get her own hands dirty. She was BOSS, and while there was often a genuine sort of rapport between her and her household staff, she trusted them not one iota. For as long as she remained in Africa, their relationship remained very much that of mistress and servant.

Not for her the horrors of close association with 'the natives' as demonstrated by such earlier eccentrics as Mary Kingsley. Nor had she any wish whatsoever to explore the interior forests or the surrounding countryside like the indomitable Miss Kingsley. If she ever left the bounds of her compound it was to go to the European Club with her husband or to the Residency for dinner. The very thought of paddling up and down rivers for months on end in dug-out canoes in the company of naked savages, as Miss Kingsley did, would have made her feel faint. One could have never imagined the average colonial wife in the sort of situation so eloquently described by Miss Kingsley about the time she had had to wade through a deep swamp:

'I had a frill of leeches around my neck like an astrakhan collar . . .'

The memsahib's toughness was of a different kind. It was, perhaps, more of a mental toughness than a physical one. She handled the lowering ennui of Coast life better than her husband, and she certainly handled the inevitable long separations better than he.

Through it all, she never forgot the gentility of her upbringing. Tea and cakes were served at four o'clock in the afternoon no matter how hot the day, just as she would have served them back home. Year after year she tried to grow English flowers from best English seeds brought out by her in little packets at the end of each vacation. Their singular lack of success did not discourage her in the slightest; indeed, the few dismal looking seedlings that did emerge – only to wither and die instantly as soon as they saw the barbaric conditions in which they were expected to grow – would be hailed by her as major horticultural triumphs. Each year on Empire Day the Union Flag would be hoisted and a toast offered to the reigning monarch, and with the approach of each Christmas she would begin the same preparations for the various forthcoming events as she had done in the previous year and in the years before that. It had to be as near to an English-style Christmas as she could make it. Garden boys would be despatched with cutlasses into the surrounding bush to bring back anything even vaguely resembling an 'English' Christmas tree, and the shrub would be set up in a corner of the living room and decorated with the usual Christmas tree baubles brought out from home, complete with white fairy at its crown. Christmas dinner would often be under the palm trees in the compound, with the dining guests periodically having to fish baby lizards, stick insects and other assorted insectivore out of their soup and custard. Christmas parties at the European Club would find Santa Claus, boiling to death under his carpet of whiskers and his heavy red cloak, handing out presents to the member's children while terrifying the little black children – watching from the seclusion of the hibiscus bushes outside – out of their wits.

The English traditions had to be maintained, come hell or high water. One had to admire their stubbornness – their complete belief that theirs was the correct way, the ONLY way, making it quite unnecessary for them to make any attempt to blend with this land that they ruled – without necessarily condoning their intransigence.

I came in during the swan song of the old colonial. The empire builders were still around, but they were an endangered species. The traders and the business people had always been there, of course, but now they were arriving in ever increasing numbers while the white administrators were departing in ever increasing numbers. At first, this new breed of white wives simply took over the reins of the old, trying to follow the ways of those who had gone. They had initial modest success, particularly those wives of husbands employed by the larger and already well-established business enterprises. A few even tried to out-snob the dreadnoughts of old, but it was no contest. Carbon copies are never the same as the originals, and anyway, their hearts weren't really in it. A new order was taking over. Gradually, as independence loomed ever more clearly on the horizon and blacks became more and more prominent in political and business affairs, integration – whether the whites liked it or not – became obligatory for them rather than being a matter for individual conscience or complete avoidance.

So, in the end, the dream that the Colonel's Lady had cherished through most of her African years was granted. She returned to her beloved England. But, such is the perversity of fate, it was more often than not to pine for the Africa that she had affected to despise, for she found that many of the traditions she had maintained in Africa as being quintessentially English had long since been abandoned in the land of her birth as being outdated. A new generation was taking over in her land too. But her stiff upper lip never quivered. She remained English to the end, and even absorbed into her daily routine the sundowners and all the other colonial niceties that had been so much a part of her life for so long . . .

If the Colonel's Lady had had problems adjusting to the changes in the Dark Continent, the indigenous Judy O'Grady experienced no such difficulty. There was a good reason for this: nothing at all had changed for her. Male chauvinism has always been alive and well in Africa. She was still one of a harem of wives for whichever chief happened to possess sufficient wealth to pay her dowry, and she still faithfully carried her husband's bath water up the hill from the stream each morning and evening. She waited on him hand and foot, and woe betide her if she ever stepped out of line. If she failed to bear him a child within a year of her marriage she could be returned in ignominy to her parents and the dowry would have to be returned to her husband. Not much chance of Girl Power flowering in this sort of environment, one would be tempted to think.

One would be wrong. Girl Power existed, all right. It was just that it was a different sort of Girl Power. It is true that the wives were the ones who did the real work in the home and in the farm, but it was rarely the man who decided what they should do or how they should do it. This was controlled by the senior wife. She allocated the daily tasks to the other wives in the menage, and she it was who decided which wife should occupy the husband's bed on any given night. Should her husband have the wherewithal and the stamina and he expressed a wish to add to his nominal roll of wives, the senior wife would be delighted. The more the merrier, was always her philosophy. Another wife on strength was never a bad thing, she always felt. Not only did it boost her influence in her own home, it was also a vital element in her perennial campaign of one-upmanship against her friends. 'Funny you should ask me, dear,' would be the gist of her reply when her husband broached the subject to her, 'I have the very girl in mind for you, and I shall see her father – who just happens to be a good friend of mine – to ask if he could be persuaded to part with her.' The deal would be struck, the dowry would be paid, father and new son-in-law would toast each other's health, and everyone, one hoped, would live happily ever after.

Those who doubted the influence of the black woman on African society had only to call on any town or village market in the Coast. Here, the 'market mammy' reigned. The market mammies were marvellous ladies, and I had enormous fun with them during my time in Africa.

Sunday markets were always the busiest. To see the market mammy at her formidable best Sunday was the day for wandering around the stalls. Invariably illiterate, no one, but no one, cheated the market mammy. She knew to the last West African ha'penny how much money she had in her bank and how much money she had to get for a particular item to make even the most infinitesimal profit on it. Her faculty for bargaining would have made the average London street trader take up Holy Orders, and she could smell a newcomer to the Coast at a thousand paces. She was an absolute mine of ribald stories, and her laughter was of such volumetric intensity as to have the wildlife in the bush for five square miles around seek even deeper cover. Her fury when aroused was awe-inspiring, and the torrent of vituperation that would explode from her would remain in the memory of her luckless victim to his dying day. No one of sound mind ever tried to take advantage of the market mammy, no matter how exalted a position he claimed in society. In her own environment, she was Queen, and with a capital 'Q' at that.

I loved each and every one of them. How often have I been introduced to a potential customer with the words: 'This is my white son. Buy from me and he will bring you luck' as I sat on a stool exchanging risqué banter with some huge, fat old dear who looked as though she had stepped out of an Uncle Remus story. This was Girl Power at the pinnacle of its development, and I have never known the man brave enough to try to buck it.

The 1960s brought a new type of Girl Power to the Coast.

Suddenly, every country along the shores of the Gulf of Guinea swarmed with very young white people who shook hands with everyone, especially if they were of sufficiently dark complexion and indigenous to that part of the world. These whites insisted on being called names such as Bugsy, Hank, Carol-Sue and Felicity-Jane. These were members of the newly formed voluntary service organizations from the United States, Canada and Britain who had been sent out to the Third World in teaching capacities. Prominent among them were the American Peace Corps.

It is doubtful if an invasion of polar bears could have created a greater stir, especially in the more remote areas. Not for John F Kennedy's elite the crisply tailored aloofness of the old colonial master, who rarely shook hands with anyone except his wife and the Governor General, and who had certainly never expressed the slightest desire to be called Bugsy or Hank by any damned native. These newcomers talked to everyone, and they often dressed even more casually than the humblest of night watchmen.

To their students, they were manna from heaven. This was a whole new slant on the world of the white man and it was one that they liked. They copied everything about these strange young whites – their jargon, their mannerisms, their total distaste for authority. Almost overnight, American ghetto-blasters were carrying the music of Chubby Checker to places where previously the only sound to offend the aural senses had been the croaking of hornbills among the umbrella trees. Suddenly Mr Hugh Hefner's ecdysic goddesses were looking a whole lot more interesting to the youth of Africa than those grotesque wooden images their fathers used to haul them off to prostrate before when the moon was riding high over the forest.

Predictably, perhaps, the older generation of African was much less impressed. He and she were the strictest of disciplinarians, and this active encouragement of freedom of expression among their children at school inevitably led to a certain amount of conflict in the home. Children were soon to learn that, while they might be on gratifyingly informal terms with their white American teacher at school, the greeting 'Hiya, pops' to their father in the home environment would be certain to result in the beating of a lifetime.

Occasionally, I came across these young volunteers in my travels. My own feelings about them were somewhat less censorious. I liked many of those I met, and – especially in later years when their organization had got its act together – some did sterling work in the most trying of circumstances. However, there was no doubt that the female volunteers I encountered were, without exception, red-hot feminists. Some were more red-hot than others. In this latter category could be placed Abbie, a tall, good-looking Anglophobe from Kalamazoo who had been posted to Pa Wilson's chiefdom.

I lived not far from Pa Wilson's village and he and I had become good friends. Because of its rather isolated nature, the village had never been much visited by the outside world, and as the only white woman for many miles around, Abbie attracted quite a lot of attention. Her scandalous views on female emancipation attracted even more attention among the Africans.

There was no noticeable rapport between her and the chief. Pa Wilson had many commendable traits, but he was no feminist. He was quite fond of the opposite sex and he had 13 wives to prove this fact, but the excitement generated by the suffragist movement in more enlightened lands had, by and large, passed him by.

One of his sons, an Oxford graduate, had returned home to marry by 'Native Law and Custom' as decreed by his tribe. According to the tribal law, normal practice for any man wishing to take a wife was to pay the father of the girl a dowry of one cow and four goats, but as a man who had achieved considerable local fame through his success overseas, young Wilson felt that he owed it to his people to put on a show of some opulence for them. Thus it was that the bride's father became the gratified – if astonished – recipient of four cows along with the standard four goats in payment for his daughter's hand in marriage.

I knew the bride-to-be well, and I was delighted to be included among her wedding guests. Abbie had not been so lucky, so, as she had not yet seen an African wedding, she prevailed upon me to use my influence to get her the necessary invitation.

She was enjoying herself hugely during the festivities until she heard about the dowry. Immediately, all that was feminist within her erupted. Having scorched the unfortunate bridegroom with the pyrotechnics of her tongue, she rounded on Pa Wilson. 'Don't you think it disgraceful,' she stormed, 'that your English-educated son should have paid four cows for his wife?'

'Indeed I do, madame,' replied Pa Wilson aggrievedly. 'But that is the younger generation for you. They will not listen to their elders. I told him that there was no woman in the whole wide world worth four cows . . .'

White Girl Power, one could not help but feel, was operating on the stoniest of ground around Pa Wilson's patch.

Chapter 8

OLD MAN AFRICA

Even then, when we first met as young men somewhere in the heart of the rainforest, he was known by no other name. If he had ever had another, no one seemed to know it and he never divulged it, not even to me when we later became very good friends indeed.

We met quite by chance. The last rays of the setting sun were lancing through the forest canopy as I hurried along a well-worn elephant track, hurrying without any real hope of reaching my survey camp before it became too dark to see. Not for the first time, so absorbed had I been in whatever I had been doing, that the end of another African day had caught me completely by surprise. There was no moon at this time of the year and, having foolishly left my torch back in camp, I was gloomily aware of the probability that I should have to spend the night huddled among the buttresses of one of the columnar obeche trees growing in such profusion here. It was harmattan time, so the nights were chilly. I did not look forward to the prospect.

I was skirting yet another of the huge, silver-barked boles when I all but stepped on him.

He was sprawled on his back on the ground, hidden from view behind one of the thin, high buttresses of the tree. A musket of extreme antiquity was propped against the trunk by his head and an elderly, very dead, mangabey monkey lay beside him. He looked up at me, grinning from ear to ear, a thin film of grey smoke curling upward from the crudely-fashioned cigarette in his hand.

'You are on the move later than usual today,' he remarked in the vernacular by way of greeting.

'How do you know that?' I riposted. 'I can't remember seeing you before.'

He drew deeply on his cigarette and spat with commendable accuracy at a lone driver ant seeking to investigate the monkey.

'No, but I have often seen you!' he informed me cryptically.

I studied him carefully. He had a wizened face, wrinkled and black as a prune. But he was not old – his body had the firmness and lustre of youth. He was as scrawny as a marabou stork and his face had a lugubrious expression that lit up like a beacon whenever he smiled, which – as I was later to find out – was often. He was, like all the forest people, barefoot, and indeed the only thing he was wearing was a singularly grubby pair of tattered shorts of indeterminate hue draped around his skinny loins. He was in dire need of a good bath; his legs were plastered with stinking swamp mud and his shoulders were caked with blood and gore and tufts of grizzled hair from the dead monkey.

'Where are you going now?' I asked him. He yawned and stretched, then scratched himself luxuriantly. He nipped out his cigarette, tucking the remaining stub with great care into a recess in his shorts. 'My camp is nearer than yours,' he said. 'I think you should spend the night with me. There is plenty of water, and we'll have monkey for dinner.'

He stood up abruptly, not waiting for my reply. He shouldered the mangabey without another word and I picked up his musket. He started off into the forest, moving away from the trail I had been using. Then he stopped and turned around, half-facing me.

'My name,' he said, 'is Old Man Africa.'

We met from time to time after that and I came to look forward more and more to his company. He was one of the most remarkable people I have ever known. Completely illiterate, he was nevertheless an accomplished raconteur, and the long African nights passed swiftly and pleasantly by the camp fires in his presence. His stories, of an age and a way of life that was even then slipping fast away from us, had me enthralled.

He was a loner, as all real hunters are, and, despite his comparative youth, he was already a master of his trade. Although he had a wife and a smattering of children, he was an indifferent father, visiting them only when the humour was on him. In all the years that I knew him, he took me but once to see his family in their village far away on the fringe of the forest, a neat little encampment of some half-dozen huts with walls of bark and roofs of palm thatch. Bananas and plantains and patches of yam grew behind it, and tall palm trees from which the villagers extracted oil and kernels for sale and barter. Scrawny chickens scratched a seemingly impossible living from the dust of the compound, and satanic-eyed goats gazed lecherously from the shadows.

His wife, a huge, jolly-looking mammy, cooked our evening meal behind her hut. All the village children turned out to stand in a semi-circle in front of us, staring round-eyed and silent, fascinated by their first sight of a white man. We lay back in our bush chairs drinking our palm wine and watched the flights of chattering, whistling grey parrots swift-winging their way high overhead to their roosting places in the tall cotton trees down by the Great River.

To me, it seemed a haven of tranquillity, a place that a man might be happy to call home. But to Old Man Africa, 'home' meant being in the depths of the forest beside some moss-banked stream, with only the dawn call of the guenon monkeys to disturb his dreams. He was in love with his hunting and the solitude of the bush and with nothing else.

He was under contract to a logging company to supply them with meat for their workers. The timber men were not too fussy what they ate and consequently an incredible assortment of antelopes, cane-rats, wild pigs, guinea-fowl, monkeys, pythons, monitor lizards and so on, found their way into the kitchens of the logging camp. These were early days in the great timber stampede and the soon-to-be ubiquitous chainsaws and tractors, with their racket and their stench, had yet to make their impact. The forests were full of wildlife and, to the black man, wildlife meant meat. The forest African was a highly carnivorous creature and a hungry Ibo axeman could consume an awful lot of meat after a hard day of felling among the huge mahoganies of the Coast.

That Old Man Africa, considering the inadequacy of what he had to work with, could keep this hungry horde satisfied, was nothing short of remarkable. Back then when we first met, his sole armament was a dane gun. Even when in prime condition this was an appalling weapon. It was highly inaccurate and often presented as great a peril to the hunter as to the intended victim. It was a primitive type of muzzle-loader with a very long barrel − often as much as five feet in length − and it was fired by a cap. The hunter loaded it with just about anything available − old nails, gravel, steel bolts, ball bearings, bits of broken cooking pot − anything at all guaranteed to kill or maim. The weapon was generally held at arm's length by the person aiming it. There were good reasons for this prudence. It had a kick like a mule, which could easily result in a shattered collar bone if it was held against the shoulder in the conventional way. There was also a very genuine fear of the barrel bursting and decapitating the owner as a result of the unorthodox material fired through it. Equally, there was the threat that the owner would find himself permanently blinded by the 'backfire' from the unpredictable firing piece. Old Man Africa's gun was no better than most; indeed, it was in an extremely dilapidated condition. It was held together with bits of liana, and I was quite convinced that only his strong faith in the god of all hunters kept him from an early and messy demise of his own making.

Chance eventually obtained for him a brand new, modern shotgun. After a series of quite fruitless complaints to the timber company about the deteriorating condition of his musket, he happened to be delivering meat to the camp kitchens one day when a garden labourer arrived posthaste to beseech his help in getting rid of a cobra which had been observed crawling high up among the fronds of a palm tree growing in the managerial compound. It was obviously only on the prowl for bird nests but, aware of the innate horror that their boss had for reptiles of any kind, they felt it wiser to dispose of the brute before it ventured any nearer to his house.

Old Man Africa had some initial difficulty in locating the snake owing to the height of the palm tree and the density of the crown.

When he eventually did catch a glimpse of it, he knew that his only chance of dislodging it would be to fire a shot blindly into the thicket of fronds and hope for the best. He pointed his musket skyward.

The thunderous discharge was followed by a shower of broken branches and other debris cascading to the ground, accompanied by a writhing black coil of large and very agile cobra. The snake hit the ground with a wallop and, apparently unscathed, unwound itself instantly and headed off at high speed across the compound, scattering the gawking crowd of spectators in all directions. As the frantic creature shot across the grass, the outdoor lavatory to the rear of the manager's house attracted its attention as a possible sanctuary from the lunatics who were trying to murder it. Like a black streak, eight feet of highly charged cobra vanished into this building through a convenient rat-hole at the back.

A split second later the Great Man himself exploded from the outhouse like a cork from a champagne bottle, minus his trousers and giving tongue lustily, moving with a fluency that belied his corpulence in a headlong stampede for the safety of his bungalow.

In very short order Old Man Africa had his new shotgun, a gleaming 12-bore of Belgian make with a glossy walnut butt. With it came a supply of cartridges and a terse directive from head office that he should clear the bush surrounding the managerial compound of all reptilian life before resuming his normal duties.

As often as work permitted, I followed Old Man Africa on his peregrinations around the forest. It was not that I was really a terribly enthusiastic hunter myself; like P G Woodhouse, I had long felt that the attraction of shooting depended very much upon which end of the weapon one happened to be standing when the trigger was squeezed. I liked the creatures of the wild too much to derive any pleasure at all from their slaughter. When I did have to hunt, it was strictly on the 'one for the pot' principle, and even then I would usually try, rather cravenly, to delegate this onerous chore to others. But I had a natural affinity for wild and lonely places, and this seemed to make me acceptable company for Old Man Africa.

As a boy, I had learned much of the ways of the countryside in my native Scotland from my woodsman father. From him, I had learned to read the tracks made by different animals and birds in mud and snow, and he had taught me every possible way to take rabbit, hare and deer on moorland and in copse. He had also instilled in me certain necessary skills in the art of evading landowners and their acolytes who, for their own selfish reasons, felt that they had a far greater claim to what moved over their land than we had. All these things I learned from him, and a good deal more besides. But Old Man Africa completed my education.

I was a willing pupil. One important difference between poaching in Scotland and hunting in Africa that soon became evident was that, while an elementary mistake in forbidden territory on my native heath would have resulted in, at worst, an unscheduled meeting with the very people one had been at pains to avoid, in the jungles of West Africa the slightest error of judgement could mean death in one of its more unpleasant forms.

I learned to read signs in the forest as easily as a surveyor reads a map. I learned how to identify an animal by a single strand of hair stuck to a twig, and how to handle a leaf as though it were of the most fragile porcelain from the tomb of a long-lost Pharaoh, comparing the amount of dew on it with that which was on adjacent leaves in order to estimate how long it had been since last disturbed. Old Man Africa knew the rainforests of the White Man's Grave better than he knew his wife, and he taught me many of its legendary secrets. He told me why the python, after killing its prey, always travels in a wide circle round its victim before attempting to swallow it, why elephants make their mysterious 'playgrounds' far inside the secluded heart of the forest, and why columns of driver ants march into fire when they encounter it on their route, committing suicide *en masse* in the flames.

He gave me a pretty good grounding on the harsher facts of life in the forest too. He told me that there were only two creatures that were quite unafraid of man – the spitting cobra and the buffalo. Give them a wide berth whenever possible, he exhorted.

'What if I cannot avoid them?' I objected.

'If a cobra comes at you,' he replied in the vernacular, 'run like hell. No snake can outspeed a fit man on open ground. But always carry a machete for protection; in a thick tangle of undergrowth the odds are on the cobra and a close encounter with an angry cobra is often fatal.'

'And the buffalo?' I queried.

Old Man Africa thought for a moment or two before he spoke. 'A meeting with a buffalo in thick bush is always memorable,' he said, 'because the buffalo has a permanent grudge against life. It is rarely more than 20 yards away from you when you first see it, and you cannot be expected to know what it is going to do next because it has no idea itself at that particular moment. Eight times out of 10 it may turn round and go about its business after scaring you half to death with its stamping and mad-eyed glowering. So it is better to stand perfectly still until it has decided, hopefully, that you are not worth bothering about.'

A wounded buffalo, he told me, was just about the most vindictive animal on earth. It would always wait in ambush for its persecutor. He taught me a useful hunting trick to avoid any unpleasant confrontation of this sort, and it was one that probably saved my life on more than one occasion. Even in the thickest of bush, the first few inches of the stems tended to be bare of leaves, so a wise precaution when suspecting an ambush was to lie flat on the ground every so often and study the land ahead. In this way the prudent hunter would have a reasonably clear view of up to 20 yards ahead, enough to reveal the feet of any motionless assassin.

He knew all there was to know about native medicines too, and from him I learned many of the secrets of the witch doctor. He told me that snuff made from the dried leaves of the red-barked dah tree, when blown from the hand, would carry a message to a distant friend. I was shown how to boil the bark of the legendary sasswood to extract a dark-brown sort of syrup that would kill a redundant wife in 10 seconds flat, and he told me that the sap of the weirdly-shaped ozouga tree, when mixed with palm wine, made such a powerful aphrodisiac that only a man of Herculean stamina and a dozen wives at his immediate disposal should attempt to use it. Of much more practical value to both of us was the knowledge that the mango-like fruit of the giant makoré made excellent cooking oil, and that the process of catching fish could be simplified by throwing pieces of mammee-apple bark into the water – toxins in the bark would stun every fish in the vicinity.

He taught me how to distinguish between the fruits and plants that were poisonous and those that were good to eat, which lianas to cut to obtain cold, clear water at the height of the dry season, and which vines to look for when malaria threatened. I also learned from him that you could not afford to be too fastidious about what you ate in the rainforest. I soon became hardened to the sight of a monkey's arm being roasted on a camp fire, and watched with feigned impassivity as the contracting sinews pulled the little fingers slowly and gruesomely into a tight fist over the flames. I ate stews made from parrots, lizards and rats, and I learned to devour with all the relish of an Edwardian gourmet dining at the Savoy, snacks of fat, white, goliath beetle caterpillars fried in rich, red palm oil.

Though admittedly sorely tempted in later years at times, I have not, so far, got round to testing the toxicity of sasswood poison on any human being, and I have never, alas, been in a situation so erotic that experiments with ozouga bark might have been beneficial to me. Nevertheless, much of what Old Man Africa taught me was put to good use during my long career in those primitive parts. I learned the art of survival in an environment that had little time for losers. And not only did I survive in a harsh world where any kind of sickness, however slight, could mean death; but on that febrile Coast, though often far from the benisons of modern medical facilities, I believe that I was fitter than ever I had been in my life.

Old Man Africa and I met intermittently over the years, sometimes by chance as in our first meeting, but, more often than not, only when he was in the mood for camp-fire gossip. Then he would seek me out and, whenever possible, I would drop whatever I was doing and follow him through the forest. There, at his lair beside some gravelly pellucid stream, we would yarn the hours away as the reflection of his fire flickered on the water's edge and the heavens sparkled and glowed in a spangled miracle of whites, jades, golds and pinks through the tangled black filigree of branches far above us.

We had many adventures together, most of them amusing in retrospect. A few were downright hair-raising. One particular encounter still gives me occasional nightmares. We had camped for the night in a small clearing dominated by a large, low-branched fig-tree. It turned out to have been a fortuitous choice of site and one that was to save our lives.

Old Man Africa had killed a swamp antelope earlier that day and the resultant stew would not have disgraced the kitchens of Paris. We lay by the fire, replete, listening to the endless churring of the cicadas and the metallic chinking of fruit bats high up in the fig-tree until, at last, sleep began to overtake us. I stood up and piled some wood on the dying fire to discourage any inquisitive leopards that might be in the vicinity. As the flames burst into life once more I turned away to follow Old Man Africa over to our stick beds under the fig-tree.

The still air of night was shattered by a fearsome bellow and we spun round in our tracks.

The sight that met our startled gaze was like a scene from the very portals of hell. A huge black buffalo stood on the edge of the clearing, steam gusting from its nostrils in twin clouds. Clods of earth flew from its hooves as it pawed the ground and glared myopically at us with all the malevolence of a questing debt collector. It lowered its head for the charge and Old Man Africa and I went up the fig-tree like squirrels.

The animal thundered through the fire like an express train, scattering embers and logs in all directions and sending showers of sparks high into the air. We watched from our roost near the top of the tree as it charged again and again, trampling the ashes into a porridge of mud before putting the final seal on its victory by triumphantly urinating on the remains of what had once been our fire.

Satisfied that it had sorted out one half of the problem, it switched the focus of its bilious gaze in our direction. The first items to attract its attention were the stick-beds and cooking gear under our tree. It took, I suppose, little more than 30 seconds to sort these out;

beds and pots were hurled into the air and strewn to the four points of the compass by the great sweeping horns.

Climbing that old fig-tree, though, had been our tactical masterstroke. The buffalo circled the sturdy trunk endlessly and with increasing irascibility, occasionally standing on its hindlegs, with forefeet propped against the bole, in vain attempts to haul us down out of there. Old Man Africa's gun was out of reach – he had lodged it in the fork of a small tree near to where we had been sitting – but, in any case, a shotgun would have been of little use against the formidable buffalo. We contented ourselves, therefore, with launching chunks of dead wood and virulent oaths down upon the head of the enraged creature, rousing it to even greater fury. It tore strips of bark from the tree with its teeth and battered the trunk with hoof and horn in a ferocity of effort that had the whole crown quivering like an aspen in a Hebridean gale.

In those upper branches to which we clung like melancholy gibbons throughout this frenetic assault, clouds of whining, stinging mosquitoes assailed us constantly and armies of fiery red tree-ants did their utmost to eat us alive as we slapped and scratched and cursed while the mad thing prowled and raged below us through that long, long night.

It was dawn before the brute left us, emptying its bowels at the foot of our tree as a last gesture of contempt before trotting off into the undergrowth, and it was another hour before we deemed it safe enough to climb stiffly down from our perch.

* * *

Old Man Africa and I were bidding each other farewell. I had been posted to another country, to a different kind of jungle, and it was unlikely that I should ever return. We yarned the hours away as we had done so many times before, laughing often at memories of the fun we had had and the exploits we had shared.

There was a lull in our conversation, an awkward silence, and we both knew it was time for me to go. The first storms of the forthcoming rains were gathering and we sat by the dying fire as Shango, the god of thunder, fretted and grumbled discontentedly to himself in the distance. A chill breeze sprang up out of nowhere, sending sparks swirling upward into the darkness in clusters of gold and silver dust.

I finished my palm wine and we stood up, just looking at each other. Then a thought struck me. 'Tell me one thing before I go,' I said. 'Have you always been called "Old Man Africa"?'

His teeth gleamed in the darkness. 'Of course not, my friend. I was a boy once, you know!'

He paused, and I waited expectantly. At last he spoke:

'My name then,' he said slowly, 'was Young Man Africa.'

Chapter 9
THE FOREST OF GHOSTS

Even to tribes far from the crags and swamps bordering this strange and beautiful land, it was known as 'The Forest of Ghosts'. Shrouded in mist for much of the year, it was rumoured that no one had ever lived in it, and certainly none had ever tried to pass through it in the memory of man. It was avoided even by the nomadic hunter, and when the palm wine flowed late at night in tiny village enclaves hidden deep in the vast forests beyond its boundaries, old men would talk in hushed voices of the grey spirits that roamed its silent woods when the moon was sleeping.

Ghosts, however, were not at the forefront of my mind as we drifted over the treetops in the tiny aircraft at the beginning of my survey. The dry season was with us, and, with the fabled mists dispersed at last, Mother Africa was garbed in her finest. A veritable network of streams sparkled through the tree canopy down below us – an intricate stitching of silver thread on a many-hued tapestry. Quartz outcrops shimmered in the morning sunshine, dazzling sentinels jutting proudly through the riot of colour that spread far and wide around them. On the lower reaches of the long escarpment, the high tops of the steel-hard eveuss trees were covered with a mantle of purple blossom, an almost garish contrast to the sombre bottle-green leaves of the giant mahoganies and walnuts higher up the slope. On the upper reaches, the towering grey-barked obeches dominated, their leaves sprinkling the great, flat crowns with a haze of delicate lime green. Scattered here and there in radiant splendour around the timbered bluffs were the squat Bombax trees which were totally bereft of leaf at this time of the year but their big, scarlet, tulip-like blossoms stood out like splashes of fresh blood against the pristine whiteness of the crags as we soared overhead.

More interesting than any to me in this extraordinary exuberance of colour, however, were the wide ribbons of shiny dark green dappled with dull beige that highlighted the banks of the meandering streams wherever I looked. The fecund mammee-apple was in fruit.

Never the most striking of trees at the best of times, in high forest the mammee-apple is forever doomed to be dwarfed by its monumental neighbours. During the hot months of January and February, however, it comes into its own, producing masses of succulent fruit, rather like rough-coated, dun mangoes in appearance. Most creatures found this fruit quite irresistible, and this annual bonanza was the signal for picnic time in the rainforest. Down below us at this very moment monkeys and parrots would be plundering the heavily laden branches, while bushbucks, chimpanzees and boisterous wild pigs would be taking care of the fallen fruit. Somewhat nervously foraging along the edges of those ribbons of green and beige would be the more reclusive of the rainforest creatures such as the chevrotain and even, perhaps, the ultra-shy bongo.

This, I felt sure, would be a wildlife paradise, a forest of beauty and solitude and the promise of adventure. But I was ever so gradually becoming aware of something else as we passed over the treetops. It was a sensation that was beginning to disturb me, a distinct feeling that something was trying to insinuate itself into my mind. My skin had suddenly become clammy and it had begun to prickle. I was aware of some strange sort of silent reverberation in the still air, like a soundless drumbeat, and it seemed to have as its source the forest beneath us, as though something – some nameless, unspeakable THING – was trying to communicate with me, sending soundless, wordless messages to me, trying to draw me down into the dark and secret depths of all this lush beauty that lay below us . . .

I glanced at the pilot beside me, but he was singing happily to himself, obviously quite oblivious of anything untoward.

I am not superstitious, but suddenly, in the fierce heat of this day, I felt an Arctic chill sweep right out through me. It was a chill that was to stay with me for the rest of the trip.

Much later that evening, when our little plane had taxied to a halt at its base in the distant city, it was with anticipation mixed with a curious sense of foreboding that I contemplated my forthcoming visit to the Forest of Ghosts.

The journey in was horrendous and my survey crew were mutinous long before the end of the first day. It was not too difficult to figure out why the Forest of Ghosts had managed to survive the ages largely untroubled by human activity. Day after awful day we slithered and stumbled, often armpit-deep, through malodorous swamp, being attacked without cessation by clouds of bloodsucking flies. Occasionally a startled cobra would veer sharply on meeting us and sail off regally through the watery sludge. Once, a huge python watched us from a low fork in a bushy mangrove. Unmoving, its cold yellow eyes fixed unwaveringly upon us as we waded cautiously past it.

The nights were even worse. As sunset approached we would dump our gear on some islet rising marginally out of the endless ooze and try to clean the mud from our aching bodies before settling down to a meal of hornbill or monkey, or indeed, anything unfortunate enough to come within range of the ancient dane gun owned by Lasana, our appointed hunter. Not that we were often hungry, in any case. Arboreal ants fell upon us from every leaf, twig or shrub we touched and the formic acid from their vicious stings inducing a lingering, unpleasant nausea within us. The onset of night was the cue for squadrons of voracious mosquitoes to batten on our blood until daylight, making sleep all but impossible. When the sun finally edged its way over the horizon to send a rippling, roseate path through the swamps towards us, it was almost with a feeling of thankfulness that we lowered our bodies once more into the foetid waters to resume our journey to the Forest of Ghosts.

At long last, though, we climbed out of the swamp and into a different world, a world of birdsong and heady perfumes. Big sand-coloured ground-squirrels scampered away from us, stopping every few yards to stand up on their hind legs and stare at us in wide-eyed astonishment. Less than a dozen yards from where we rested a sunbird perched on a flowering shrub, its long, curved beak buried in the pink fragrance. It sipped deeply of the nectar and paid no attention to us. A shaft of afternoon sunshine, dust-laden, speared through the quiet coolness, settling on the bush and the busy little bird, illuminating its plumage in all its iridescent splendour. All around us colossal mahoganies, eight feet in diameter, towered upward, like great marble pillars in a Roman amphitheatre and rose branchless for a hundred feet and more, their crowns locked in tangled embrace against a sapphire sky. In their majestic shadows grew the slender ebonies and camwoods, all of them living together in perfect harmony since time immemorial, I reflected, without any help at all from the human race.

I stood up abruptly, and the sunbird vanished in a blur of emerald and purple and vermilion and black.

We set up camp beside a stream whose waters were as cool and clear as a Hebridean burn. It was an idyllic setting. A deep pool at the foot of a little waterfall just behind our camp was soon occupied by a gang of extremely dirty workers, and I decided we should rest at this camp for a few days before beginning our survey.

The night was eerie. There was no other word for it. In Africa, nights are usually full of sound – the endless, rattling call of the tree hyrax, the mewing of civet cats, the snuffles of a wandering aardvark, the cough of a prowling leopard – but, in this forest, nothing stirred. Even the usually ubiquitous cicadas were stilled. There was no moon, and the sky was as black as ink. The crew huddled round the fire, muttering uneasily among themselves throughout the night, and I had to admit to a feeling of some relief when the sun rose to herald our first full day in the Forest of Ghosts.

In the afternoon, I left the gang loafing around the camp while I set off on a reconnaissance upstream. Kingfishers flickered in turquoise and white over the tumbling waters above the camp, and otters sported in the bigger pools with their distinctive whistling calls ringing cheerfully through the trees.

I climbed to the top of the slope and rested a while under the trees, looking through half-closed eyes up at the roof of green above me. I was in more open forest here, forest which consisted mainly of huge, semi-deciduous obeche, and through the leaves far overhead I could catch glimpses of cotton-wool clouds drifting lazily across the blue of the sky. The primitive fears of the night before seemed absurd in this lovely setting.

A harsh KEE-KEE-KEE scream startled me into wakefulness. A great crowned eagle sailed over the treetops and I leaned on my elbow, watching it. Rising then, I headed east into the forest, intending to take a different route back downhill to camp. Alas, as the poet Burns never wearied of telling us, the best laid schemes . . I had travelled no more than a couple of miles when everything happened at once: a thick mist enveloped the forest, and with it came night so rapidly that I was caught completely by surprise.

The silence of the grave swallowed me up.

Fortunately I had been standing by the massive buttresses of a tall mahogany, so just before it became too dark to see, I decided to utilize one of its deep cavities as a refuge for the night. After a precautionary banging session on the thin, high flanges with a stick to lessen the risk of encountering cantankerous tenants − such as cobras − I squeezed inside, hunched myself into a ball, and settled down to await the dawn.

The night was interminable. I was cold, damp and miserable and I jerked awake frequently. The darkness was total and the silence was complete. Twice during the night I fancied I could hear whispering sounds, as though sepulchral feet were brushing over dry leaves, but so black was the night that I could not have seen my hand had I held it in front of my face.

I woke abruptly. There was now the merest hint of light outside, more of a promise of light, perhaps, than actual light itself. I strained my eyes against the blackness as, almost imperceptibly, the shades of night began to retreat.

My heart jolted. In the thick, grey murk outside, surely there was an even darker mass of grey? And another? And another? Christ, yes! THEY were there! Huge, grey, formless silhouettes, everywhere around me . . . silent . . . motionless . . . menacing . . . The hair prickled on the nape of my neck as the stories I had heard about this place came flooding back to my mind.

I crouched for what seemed like an eternity inside my sanctuary, scarcely daring even to breathe.

The fart was sudden and explosive. It came from the grey hulk directly in front of me and in the still air it had all the percussion effect of a shot from a cannon. A ray of sunshine pierced the mist and the 'ghosts', as if on command, began to move. I was in the midst of a huge herd of elephants! Mothers, grannies, aunties, frisky youngsters – they were by the score, feeding now on the fallen mammee-apple fruit.

The Forest of Ghosts! So these were the fabled grey ghosts! I watched, fascinated, as they moved slowly forward, listened to the scrunching of mighty jaws and the gurgling of great stomachs as they gorged themselves on the sweet fruit. Only when the last straggler had disappeared into the forest did I dare to crawl out, stretch myself stiffly, and move off down the hill in the direction of my camp.

So that, you might say, solved the mystery. And yet – did it really? Even now, close to half a century later, one thing still puzzles me. It was the stillness, the eerie silence, of that herd in the night. Elephants feed by night as well as by day, you know. They have to. Their bulk is such that constant feeding is essential. Yet those elephants had stood there patiently, without movement, without sound, as immobile and mysterious as the stone statues of Easter Island, awaiting, like myself, the coming of dawn.

To this day, I wonder. What were they? Were they, in fact, phantoms by night and living, flesh-and-blood creatures by day, as camp-fire legend would have it? Or were they really elephants, but, like myself, afraid of disturbing the real keepers of the night, the silent grey shapes from another world that patrolled those woods when the moon was asleep?

Or was it all just a dream? A hallucination?

I shall never know. Within the week, my gang had deserted me, spooked by the abnormal silence of the nights and their own very African dread of the supernatural. Without workers, I had no option but to follow them out of that remarkable forest. I never returned.

The Forest of Ghosts is now but a memory. It succumbed long ago to the voracious logger.

And chainsaws are murderously pragmatic things.

Chapter 10

OSEI THE CARPENTER

Osei the Carpenter had one hour of life left, give or take a few minutes as you choose. Not that he was aware of this disturbing fact. Not yet, anyway. On the contrary, he was rather pleased with himself. For one thing, he had acquired a new and comely wife at a knockdown price, and this – to men like Osei with an eye for a bargain – was always guaranteed to buck one up. Secondly, he had been given permission by the village chief to build a hut for her.

Not all new wives were accorded this privilege. Indeed, with someone less popular than Osei this might have caused considerable friction within the village. But Osei was a good and kindly man, and he was held in high esteem, not only by his other wives, but by everyone who knew him. No one had ever been heard to say a bad word about Osei the Carpenter.

This was a little unusual, for he was not of their tribe. He was not, in fact, even of their country. He had come to the village as a young man many years ago, footsore and weary, carrying all that he possessed on his head, and he had asked their permission to stay the night. He had never left them.

No one knew from whence he had come and none had asked. This is not to say that the desire to pry into the affairs of others is any less acute among the people of the Coast than it is in more advanced societies. To claim this would be to gainsay the existence of one of the most popular village pastimes the world over, be the inhabitants black or white or brown or yellow. It is just that there are still places in this shrinking world where it is considered not only discourteous but downright dangerous to be seen to be too interested in a man's background. Some mysteries are best left unsolved.

Of course, this village being on the fringe of the rainforest and the bush telegraph therefore being as active here as anywhere else in Africa, rumours about him did filter through from time to time, most of them being so fanciful as to be patently nonsensical. The one given the greatest credence was that his father had been a famous witch doctor in a distant country who had fallen foul of the colonial authority of the day. Human sacrifice, it was whispered, had been involved, and it is a well documented fact that colonial administrators from the beginning of time have always had a horror of any menu that features *Homo sapiens* as its *pièce de résistance*. Osei, these scandalmongers had hinted, had only escaped the fate of his now defunct father by boring a hole through the mud wall of his prison one dark night and vanishing into the surrounding forest.

But rumours are no better than they are called, and, as Osei himself gave them no hint about his past, the villagers had had to be content with that. What was of much more importance to them was that he had gone out of his way from the beginning to be accepted as an integral part of their society, and so easy-going was he by nature that this did not take long.

Over the years he had acquired two wives from his adopted tribe. Both marriages had proved fruitful and his children were the joy of his heart. On one of his infrequent trips out of the bush a chance encounter with some northern cattlemen had introduced him to the teachings of Mohammed. He had embraced the Muslim faith and a tall, graceful Fulani girl called Bindu with almost equal fervour, to the temporary discombobulation of the other villagers, who were pagan to a man and intended to remain so. Their pique, however, was not of long standing, partly because of their liking for him but mainly because, by now, Osei was a man of some substance as a result of one talent that set him apart from all his peers.

Osei was a carpenter of the highest quality.

Carpenters have always been ten-a-penny in the African bush, and most of them are little better than adzemen. But Osei was different. He had a genuine love for his chosen vocation, and many's the hour and day he would spend on a single block of wood, methodically working on it until he had it carved to his satisfaction. The golden brown patina of the majestic African walnuts, the exquisitely rippled grain of the rich red mahoganies, the aphrodisiac fragrance of the rose-pink Guareas – only those born to be carpenters are capable of appreciating the sort of pleasure experienced by Osei as he whittled and smoothed the time away in his little lean-to workshop under the old mango tree at the foot of the village.

And there was no disputing the fact that Osei was a true carpenter. His name became synonymous with quality. His fame spread, and people came from far and wide to purchase his carvings and employ his services. As a result, his position in the village hierarchy had escalated gradually over the years, so that by now he had achieved a status second only to that of the chief himself.

With that, Osei the Carpenter was content. He had no further ambitions left in life. Except, of course to build a house, a splendid house of mud brick and the finest of timbers, a home worthy of the name of Osei the Carpenter, for Bindu, his beautiful new wife . . .

So he toiled away happily now in the yellow heat of noon, lifting, shoving and heaving at the heavy mahogany planks he had pitsawn and stacked here on the edge of his little farm during the previous dry season, piling on one side the sizes he required and throwing to the other side those he did not. Sweat ran down the broad slopes of his shoulders to trickle in tiny rivulets down his spine to the cleft of his buttocks, staining to a dark chocolate hue the wrap of faded khaki around his loins. He sang as he worked, sporadic and sudden volleys of sound discharged into the atmosphere in an unnerving, tuneless whine that sent overhead flights of parrots sheering away sharply in squawking alarm.

Under the timber stack, death stirred suddenly, uneasily.

The dry rustling sound went through Osei the Carpenter like the thrust of a cold spear. He straightened abruptly, every sense alert, his red-veined eyes wide and suspicious. A pulse throbbed on his neck as he stood motionless, listening . . . listening . . .

A large tombo fly zinged, unheeded, around his head. It settled on his neck and waited, antennae oscillating, on guard for the anticipated swipe of a hand. None came, and it focused its huge green eyes on the conduit of blood before it. Slowly and expertly, it sank its proboscis into the bulging artery.

From far up the hill the cracked call of a village rooster echoed faintly in the still air. Now the gentlest of zephyrs stirred the leaves of the young pepper plant beside him. The papery susurration reassured him and he relaxed, exhaling slowly. He slapped irritably at the fly and returned his attention to the task on hand.

Only the bottom tier of planks remained, set upon billets of wood to keep them clear of the wet African clay. Although barely half a year had elapsed since he had stacked them, the fecund humidity of these equatorial regions was such that this bottom layer was now cocooned in a tangled mat of thorny vines. He attacked the wiry tendrils with his machete, the broad blade spanging tinnily with each stroke.

Satisfied at last, he laid down his machete and reached for the nearest length of timber. He yanked at it, a short, grunting jerk. It did not even budge. Exasperated, he grasped the centre plank and wrenched at it with the full power of his sinewy old arms. The whole bottom deck came apart so easily and with such a splintery explosion of sound that he was caught completely by surprise. He stumbled backwards onto his rump with a resounding wallop.

From underneath what was left of the timber stack a long black coil of doom erupted and was upon him instantly, grabbing the calf of his leg in a huge pink maw, chewing at it like a dog, as cobras will, with each bite injecting enough venom to flatten an elephant.

His first high, gurgling scream brought the villagers pell-mell down the hill, but by the time they reached him it was too late. They saw the cobra disappearing into the forest like a galleon in full sail, its carmine neck puffed out angrily and held high above the ground. They saw Osei sprawled on his back, his limbs twitching gruesomely and his teeth grinning at them in a final, terrible rictus.

But Osei the Carpenter was aware of none of these things. Nor was he aware of his new and beautiful wife weeping over him. His spirit was already winging its way over the dark and turbulent waters of the River of the Dead.

In accordance with custom for those who had died of snakebite or other unnatural causes, Osei was laid to rest in the Devil Bush. This was a tract of low-lying, swampy forest a few miles from the village. It was a silent, gloomy place, home to clouds of mosquitoes by night and voracious tsetse flies by day. Snakes of many kinds infested it, and legions of the little brown rats that they fed upon. Great hairy spiders lay in wait behind vast, sticky webs, webs that were strong enough to stop a man in his tracks. It was a singularly horrible piece of bush, forbidden to all except the witch doctor and his burial parties. It was, in any case, a place no human being in his right mind would want to venture anywhere near.

This sepulchral place, legend would have it, was frequented by the souls of the dead. Spectral figures, it was said, could be seen moving over its foetid waters by day and by night, ghouls in ceaseless quest for the unwary to enfold within their cold, eternal embrace . . .

As I stood on a small hill overlooking the Devil Bush in the coolness of evening, watching the little band of pallbearers move slowly into the anonymity of its dank shadows with the mortal remains of Osei the Carpenter, I found it not too difficult to believe at least some of what I had heard. I promised myself there and then that, wherever my travels might take me in the future, I would endeavour to ensure that the swamps of the Devil Bush were not included in my itinerary.

I had known Osei well, and I had purchased carvings from him on a number of occasions over the years. With his demise my reason for visiting the village had gone. It was, in fact, to be another two years before I had occasion to visit the area again, and I was well on my way to the village when I realized that the path I was following, while not actually passing through the Devil Bush itself, would certainly take me along the perimeter of it.

Now, I do not regard myself as being particularly superstitious, although I have seen things happen in the depths of the African bush for which even men of science could offer no feasible explanation. But, on the other hand, I am no more fond of haunted places than the next person. In normal circumstances I would have taken time to find an alternative route. But today I was in a hurry; the evening shadows were fast lengthening and I was anxious to reach the village before the onset of night.

I hastened along the boundary of that weird place, keeping to the dry slopes skirting it, chillingly aware of the crypt-like quiet that permeated the mist-wreathed swamp vegetation below me. I saw not one single living creature, and the only thing to be heard as I hurried on my way was the sound of my own footsteps scuffing through the dead leaves on the path.

A movement far in front of me caught my attention and I came to a halt. The figure of a woman was moving slowly down the path in my direction. She was balancing a large pan on her head and it was piled high with yams and plantains. Puzzled as to why anyone should be carrying provisions in the vicinity of this forbidden bush, I waited for her. She walked unhurriedly, sedately, her eyes lowered and her skirt sweeping the ground regally behind her, like some Hamitic princess from Pharaonic times. About 20 yards from me she stopped and looked up.

'Bindu!' I exclaimed, startled.

Osei the Carpenter's wife stood before me. She was looking at me and through me, unseeing, her eyes milky-white in her once-lovely face. She was completely blind.

I opened my mouth to say something, but she beat me to it. 'You are the white man who used to buy things from Osei the Carpenter.' It was not a question; it was a statement, and I knew the ways of the forest better than to ask how, with her blindness and with no way immediately discernible to me that she could have been aware of my coming, she had known instantly who I was. I waited for her to continue. 'I am taking food to my husband,' she said simply. 'He is building a house for me in the Devil Bush.'

I was too stunned to say anything. She turned off the path,

heading down the hill to the Devil Bush, following a little game trail so indistinct as to be virtually invisible, but which she trod with the confidence of one who knew precisely where she was going. At the edge of the swamp she turned to face me. She was smiling, and it was a smile of the purest serenity and joy. Her face, framed against the deep shadow of the Devil Bush, seemed to have an eerie luminosity about it. She was, I realized with sudden shock, quite mad.

'Take care how you walk, white man,' she said. 'You may meet Osei the Carpenter on the path in front of you.'

Then she was gone into the blackness of the swamp.

If I had been in a hurry before, I was in an even greater hurry now. My feet fairly flew over the ground, and it was with a sense of profound relief that I finally approached the point where the path parted company with this spooky place to meander through the timbered valley beyond to the clean fresh air of the hills around the village.

I rounded the corner and stopped abruptly, my heart doing violent flip-flops within me.

A few yards in front of me an enormous spitting cobra was slowly crossing the path, making for the Devil Bush. It saw me and instantly reared up, its vivid red hood flaring its lethal warning at me. Its black bootlace of a tongue flicked in and out as it waited, coiled and motionless, on the path before me. Its little eyes, cold and expressionless as the brown glass eyes of a voodoo doll, stayed locked on mine for what seemed an eternity. Finally, having appeared to decide that I was harmless, it deflated its hood noisily, lowered its head to the ground, and slid on its way with sibilant smoothness into the Devil Bush.

I stood there for some time after it had gone, my shirt soaked with clammy sweat, trying to calm my jangling nerves, not daring to try to put any possible significance to this latest encounter. As the pounding of my heart gradually eased I became aware of a tapping sound, an increasingly intrusive tac-tac-tac . . . tac-tac-tac . . . from deep within the swamp. It was too slow and erratic to be that of woodpeckers at work, although it had much the same tonal resonance.

There was something disturbingly hypnotic about it, and, though some inner voice screamed at me to rapidly put as much distance between myself and this accursed place as possible, my body was powerless to obey. The siren call of the swamp seemed to beat stronger, ever stronger . . . TAC-TAC-TAC . . . TAC-TAC-TAC in my head, willing me forward. As in a trance, I found myself walking slowly down the slope to the edge of the Devil Bush.

I peered into the murk, trying to locate the source of the tapping. At first I could see nothing at all, but gradually my eyes became accustomed to the darkness. Swamp water bubbled treacly everywhere I looked, and the whole area was an impenetrable morass of every conceivable species of swamp growth — stunted abura trees, stilt-rooted Macarangas, smothering tangles of liana, and low-branching raffia palms that spread their straggly, spiny fronds every which way above and below the surface of the water.

The tapping stopped, and now a deathly hush hung over the Devil Bush. I was rooted to the spot, quite unable to tear myself away from this awful place. Far out in the swamp, a light flickered. It was the faintest of lights, dim and bluish, such as one might have expected from a smoky lantern, and it was moving slowly and aimlessly in the heart of the swamp, backwards and forwards, backwards and forwards, above the surface of the water. I watched it as it zigzagged back and forth, but I could see no sign of anyone with it. Then I saw another, and another, appearing out of nowhere, moving ever so casually but with nonetheless perceptible sureness in my direction. Suddenly there were dozens of them, cold blue lights, jigging in phantasmic dance formation, moving faster and faster and faster, over the black waters towards me. I found my voice at last in a yell of sheer terror, a cry that echoed out through the swamp, and a great grey heron exploded from a clump of reeds close by me, croaking harshly, indignantly, its long neck outstretched and its cumbersome wings beating noisily as it strained its scrawny body upward, up and out of this hellish mire towards the sanctuary of the evening stars.

The spell was broken. I turned and fled, back up the slope, bolting in frantic, headlong flight, away from the horrors of the Devil

Bush and out through the shifting shadows of the towering mahoganies, up the winding trail to the distant village.

I sat with the village chief outside his hut. The sun had long since gone but there was still a hint of its valedictory splendour to be seen in the dark velvet of the sky to the west, a band of magenta streaked with gold and turquoise highlighting the tops of the trees on the horizon. A gibbous moon hung low over the black outline of the crags to the north. I turned to the old man.

'What has happened to the village and your people?' I asked in wonderment. Two years ago the village and been clean and prosperous. Now, of the few huts that remained intact, only two appeared inhabited, the chief's hut and that of the late Osei the Carpenter. The others stood forlorn, disintegrating. The stench of putrefaction filled the air and weeds scrambled all over the compound. The goats and sheep that used to wander freely around the village had gone and only a few miserable looking chickens remained, huddled disconsolately under the eaves behind us.

The chief began to speak. His voice was the piping, tremulous voice of a very sick old man.

Soon after Osei the Carpenter died, he began, he had taken Osei's three wives into his ménage, as decreed by tribal law. The two senior wives had come willingly enough but the youngest, Bindu, was still distraught with grief. In addition, said the chief, she had foolish Muslim ideas about fidelity and had had to be forced into sharing his bed. Two days later, while out working on the chief's farm, she had come upon a large cobra which had instantly discharged its venom full in her face, blinding her.

'She went crazy from that day onward,' the old man went on, 'And she said it was Osei's punishment on her for coming to my bed. She said that a curse would fall upon the village and that I would die if I did not move her back to Osei's house. So I did as she asked, and she has stayed there ever since.'

'And the other villagers?' I interjected.

'A week later,' the chief continued, 'A terrible sickness came to our village. It visited the huts one by one, giving a bad fever to every man, woman and child, making them mad, blinding them, killing them. One after another they were carried off to the Devil Bush. Some ran away from the village, and Osei's senior wives and children went with them. Now, only I and my senior wife remain. And the youngest wife of Osei the Carpenter.'

I thought about my encounter with Bindu. 'I met her by the Devil Bush today,' I said. 'What do you think she might have been doing there?'

'The sickness only touched her,' he mumbled evasively, 'And although she is a bit mad, I cannot drive her away, for she still belongs to Osei the Carpenter.'

I tried to ignore the implication in his answer. Still searching desperately for a mundane reason for everything, I said: 'She is mad, for true! She believes that Osei is still alive!'

The old man was gazing into the night, out to the silhouettes of the distant hills. I pondered upon how very frail he had become in the two years since I had last seen him. He spoke again. 'Did you see anything else when you were down by the Devil Bush?'

'I saw one mighty cobra,' I told him. 'It was going into the Devil Bush. And,' I continued with an involuntary shiver, 'I saw lights moving around inside the swamp.'

He sat in silence for a long time, resting his back against the wall of the hut and looking up into the night sky. Far off in the forest a tree hyrax kick-started itself into action with its strange, interminable call, a bloodcurdling, rattling cry, like that of a child being throttled. The call echoed eerily around the surrounding bluffs and hung with throbbing intensity in the still air of the village compound.

At last, he whispered: 'Osei the Carpenter! The snake you saw was Osei the Carpenter!'

I said nothing, remembering the strong snake cult tradition that existed among the tribes of the Coast. He went on: 'Osei's spirit is with the snake. Just before my people took sick and died, the snake entered every house in the village. Every hut except my one. One night soon it will come to my place, and then I will join Osei the Carpenter in the Devil Bush.'

He reached across and put his hand on my knee. His face was only inches from my own. His eyes gleamed with a peculiar silvery light in the moonlight. It was then that I realized that he, too, was completely mad.

'Osei the Carpenter,' he said, gazing into my eyes with the fixed intensity of the mentally unbalanced, 'is building a house in the Devil Bush. When it is built, the snake will come for us. And he will take us with him to the Devil Bush. You and me and my senior wife. And the wife of Osei the Carpenter.'

He took his hand away from my knee and resumed his demented vacuous contemplation of the dark void of the heavens, staring through space and time towards the distant galaxies. Far off in the vast mysterious forest the strangled scream of the hyrax rose to a staccato crescendo.

*   *   *

'Lassa fever! Nothing ghostly about it! Just an epidemic of Lassa fever!' said my eminent medical friend brusquely many years later when I told him the story of Osei the Carpenter. 'A serious viral disease, thought to be spread by rats. Only properly identified in 1969, but it has been around for donkey's years. Not a lot known about it, except that it is characterized by very high fever, quite often followed by blindness, dementia and death.'

We were sitting in the plush surroundings of one of the larger hotels in London, a far cry from the swamps of the Devil Bush. He had practised for many years in West Africa himself, and he had made a detailed and objective study of the misty world of the witch doctor. I was now on vacation, visiting him.

'But it was Osei's death that sparked off the whole chain of events,' I pointed out. 'How do you account for that?'

'Sheer coincidence!' replied my ever-pragmatic friend. 'Osei's death and what happened afterwards were nothing but unrelated coincidence. Osei was killed by a cobra. The village was wiped out because it was plagued by viral-carrying rats. Simple as that! And snakes are attracted to human habitation in the African bush because of the vermin they find to eat there. The cobra was only after the rats that were spreading the disease in the first place.'

'But that cobra,' I persisted, 'it killed Osei, it blinded Bindu and drove her mad, it was blamed for the destruction of a whole community, and it damn near scared me into a decline two years later on the edge of the Devil Bush. Surely this is stretching the long arm of coincidence a bit far?'

He lifted his glass and stirred the amber fluid absently. 'That might have been so, had everything been precisely as you have described,' he said meditatively. 'But perhaps it is worth reflecting on this: except to the eyes of the experienced herpetologist, one large cobra tends to be very much like another. Spitting cobras are common throughout West Africa. It would seem reasonable to assume that Osei's cobra was, in fact, several cobras. The rat and lizard population around the Devil Bush and the village would have been enough to sustain a sizeable army of them.'

I was still not satisfied. 'What about the lights I saw in the Devil Bush?'

He grinned smugly across the table at me. 'Ignis fatuus!' he said succinctly.

'What?'

'Ignis fatuus. "Will-o'-the-Wisp" to you! You sometimes get it in swampy areas where there is an abundance of decaying vegetable matter. The rotting material produced methane, and this can be ignited by the traces of hydrogen phosphide that you often find in association with such sites. You must have read about it at school – it used to scare the hell out of the reivers from your country in the bad old days when they had to cross the Solway bogs to do their pillaging in England.'

It all seemed so simple, so easy to explain as I sat in that elegant cocktail bar, that I could not think why I had not figured it out for myself in the first place. Even the tapping sounds I had heard in the Devil Bush – which, in my overheated frame of mind on that strange evening long ago, I had taken to be the sound of nails being hammered into planks by a phantom carpenter – could now be explained away as having been some perfectly natural phenomenon such as, perhaps, chimpanzees breaking open coula nuts with stones.

'Correct!' said my friend when I mentioned this to him. 'Just mere coincidence again. But because it fitted the scenario you had already had imprinted in your mind, you were ready to believe anything. People who visit haunted houses are there to find ghosts. They are disappointed if none materialize. You knew the reputation of the Devil Bush, so you were more prepared to accept the illogical than the logical. Had Osei himself come into your room the night you stayed with the chief, you would not have been in the least surprised.'

He rose and went over to the bar to order another round. I settled back in my chair and stared at the chandeliers. He was right, of course. It had all been fantasy. His clinical mind had effectively laid the ghost of Osei the Carpenter.

But I wouldn't go back to that Devil Bush if you paid me a king's ransom.

Chapter 11
MAGIC SPERM

He had travelled far in the back of a mammy wagon to see me, and the blackness of his skin was dusted a greyish pink from the laterite clays of old Africa. He stood before my desk now, an insignificant little runt of perhaps 14 years of age clad only in a pair of disreputable khaki shorts several sizes too large for him.

I had spread the word around that I was looking for a clerk for a tree survey I was about to conduct in a remote area of forest and it was a job that would require a comprehensive knowledge of trees and a reasonable standard of written English. Applicants had been few; most bush people knew their trees, all right, but those who had the necessary standard of literacy refused point blank to venture into remote forests among strange and possibly hostile tribes, not to mention even more hostile creatures. Less hazardous clerical work was easily obtainable nearer to home.

'Do you know trees?' I asked.

'My father is a hunter,' he replied proudly, 'and we live in the forest. I know all the trees.'

'You would not be afraid to travel with me to faraway places?'

'No sir.'

I studied him carefully. He had no tribal markings on his face, but he had that alert wiriness about him that seemed to be the hallmark of so many Ekitis.

'Can you write and count?' I enquired.

'Yes, sir. I attended the Sacred Heart Catholic School in Ekiti for five whole years.'

'But can you write good English?' I persisted doubtfully. 'After only five years at school?'

'Dem Reverend Fadders get dam' strong arm, sir,' he replied emphatically.

I had made up my mind. 'I want to see how well you can write,' I said finally. 'Write me a letter of application for this job and bring it to me in the morning. If I'm satisfied with that, you're hired.'

He was heading for the door when I called after him: 'By the way, what is your name?'

He turned in the doorway. 'My name, sir,' he informed me with the quiet dignity of his race, 'is Magic Sperm.'

I suppose his name should have given me some hint of what was to follow. But, apart from musing upon the absurdity of it and wondering idly how he had acquired it, I gave little thought to the matter at the time. Exotic sobriquets were common in the forests of the White Man's Grave in my day. I already had on strength a Local Thunder, a Money-No-Reach and a Two-At-One-Time. Probably, I conjectured, he had seen it on the label of a bottle of virility potion in a bazaar somewhere and had adopted it without understanding its significance.

His letter of application, when he brought it the following morning was couched in the quaintly florid English invariably employed by those who had served time in mission schools in the African hinterland. It began: 'Dear Master, I have long admired you from afar, and now I wish to satisfy you on the ground . . .' and it ended: 'May God have mercy on your soul, Yours lovingly, Magic T Sperm.'

I never did find out what the 'T' stood for.

He was good at the job for which I had hired him. It did not, it has to be admitted, involve anything of a very physical nature insofar as he was concerned: all he had to do was jot down in his notebook the species and girth of trees called out to him by the tree-finders as we cruised out through the forest. But he had a most engaging personality. He was willing and he was cheerful, absolutely bubbling with *joie de vivre*, to the extent that even the gloomiest of forests seemed to brighten when he was around.

Having someone like Magic Sperm in the gang when they were operating far from home for lengthy periods was an invaluable asset. The African bush man was rarely at ease when too long away from his own tribal territory. We could be away for varying periods, anything from one month to ten weeks or even more, but it never seemed to bother Magic Sperm. On reflection, I doubt if it would have bothered Magic Sperm if he had suddenly found himself in the middle of the rush hour in Piccadilly Circus. His disposition was so carefree that he just took life as it came, whatever the traumas.

I had only a small crew of about a dozen men with me, and we lived pretty much off the land. One of the workers, a tall Hausa lad called Lasana, was a good hunter. When he first came to me, he was the proud possessor of an incredibly old and dangerous looking musket. He was delighted when I obtained a modern, single-barrelled shotgun for him, and he kept us well supplied with antelope and guinea fowl.

Magic Sperm, it transpired, was an enthusiastic fisherman. The rainforests were criss-crossed with waterways of all descriptions, and the smallest stream was full of life. Most of the things that he caught were of such miserably small proportions that any self-respecting fisherman would have been ashamed to keep them. There was no shame whatsoever about Magic Sperm. Everything, from the tiniest of shrimps and freshwater crabs to the most repulsive of frogs, went into his soup pot.

On a trip out to one of the larger coastal towns I bought him some line and some hooks. This produced much more satisfactory results in the larger streams and rivers, even perch and carp of up to a pound in weight on occasion. He was certainly keen. Whenever he had a half day off work he would head for the nearest water and cut himself a long, green, whippy stick. He would tie the end of his line around the butt close to his hand for security in case some large fish broke his rod, then he would carefully wind the rest of the line around the tip. His favourite bait was the big green grasshoppers that could be found in profusion along the banks of any West African waterway.

Immediately they were touched they ejected a vile smelling fluid, but this did not bother Magic Sperm in the slightest. He would pull the wings off them so that they would float just below the water surface rather than on it – he maintained that this method gave the best results – and he would sit for hours by the water, as patient as a heron, waiting for that tell-tale pull on his line.

Once, he baited his hook with a live chameleon. God alone knows what took it, but chameleon, line and rod shot off downstream at a remarkable rate of knots, and Magic Sperm would probably have vanished along with them had the rod not been wrenched so fiercely and suddenly out of his hands.

Once, too, while I was with him, he caught an enormous black catfish which lay on the bank glaring evilly at us and croaking horridly. Magic Sperm and the gang ate it happily that night but I had temporarily lost my appetite for fish and I opened a tin of corned beef instead.

I never learned very much about his family. I did not meet any of them, but I heard bits and pieces about them from the other workers. His father, being a hunter, lived a rather nomadic life and he was rarely at home. (He must, one presumed, have been at home on 16 separate occasions, for Magic Sperm had been his sixteenth child.) Magic Sperm was much more willing to talk about his grandmother. She was, he told me, a herbalist in Idanre, a small town nestling among spectacular rock formations to the south of Ado-Ekiti. Each time we were due to leave our area of work and return to our home base he would carry out a sackful of bark, roots, tree resin, leaves, seeds, dried insects and all kinds of other unidentifiable junk for her little shop. She was, by all accounts, something of a legend in her area and he told me that he was very proud of her, for had she not in her youth fatally poisoned a prominent local politician?

I warmed to the old lady myself the moment I heard this story.

I think, in his own way, Magic Sperm liked the bush work almost as much as I did. It was such a free and easy existence, and it was a busy one. By the time we had cleaned up and eaten something at the end of a hard day's work there was not too much thought of indulging in youthful shenanigans. We were all too tired, and besides, the African night descended with particular rapidity when one was living in the depths of the forest. There was, in any case, nowhere to go.

The problems arose on those occasions when I had to return to headquarters, which I had to do every so often to collect wages and compile maps and reports. Magic Sperm, I was soon to discover, had a low boredom threshold. He had to be kept fully occupied, a concept easier said than applied. He proved useless in the office, and the very sight of anything resembling physical labour made him quite ill. Eventually, as the sight of his doleful figure around my office door was beginning to make me feel ill, I told him to stay away from my compound until it was time to go back to the forest.

As I was rarely at headquarters for more than a week at a time, this seemed to me to be the ideal solution. It was certainly so for Magic Sperm. He had found the perfect antidote to boredom. By the dawning of his fifteenth birthday he had impregnated more maidens during those brief visits than the King of Benin had achieved after a lifetime of trying with his extensive official harem.

Or so it seemed to me. I began to dread each homecoming, knowing that I was sure to be greeted by yet another posse of wrathful fathers, their obviously fecund daughters in tow and voices aquiver with indignation as they assailed me with their now familiar reproach: 'Massa, your Sperm Boy . . .'

I suppose it was inevitable that I should end up as the scapegoat in Magic Sperm's indiscretions. A visit to the area by one of the country's leading emergent politicians – a man noted for his brutally robust responses to those who crossed him – had been unofficially marked by a night of amorous dalliance between Magic Sperm and one of the entourage, a young lady who just happened to be the Great Man's favourite niece. The resultant unpleasantness cost me a case of best gin to placate the incensed politician and several crates of imported beer to keep his bodyguards from shooting everything in sight, myself included.

When they had departed, I went in search of Magic Sperm. His room was empty. He had packed his bag and vanished, never to return.

Six weeks later I was passing through a town some distance to the north and I called at the Catholic Girls' Grammar School on the outskirts. Convents are not places I choose to visit regularly and I cannot now remember why I should have been in this particular one, but I do remember being escorted round the premises by a nun of quite outstanding beauty.

Sister Mary – I shall call her that, though this was not her real name – was a new arrival on the Coast. She was very young and sweetly naive. She had been given charge of the convent gardens; a labour of love, she assured me, as she had always been fond of gardening back in Ireland. She liked life in West Africa, she said, even though she was experiencing the usual problems in adjusting: the sweltering heat, the smells, the flies, the difficulty in understanding the local pidgin English . . .

We stopped in the shade of a mango tree on the edge of the garden. I gazed at the figure of a youth working industriously with a hoe some distance from us. 'That,' she told me proudly,' 'is Boniface, one of my protégés. My best worker, and a leading member of our church choir.'

We wandered out through the garden, past the perspiring youth, but Magic Sperm did not look at us. We returned to the mango tree. 'How did – er – Boniface manage to get a job with you, Sister?' I asked curiously.

'He came here about six weeks ago, and I felt so sorry for him,' said the Sister. 'He told me that he had been working for a very cruel white man who beat him every day with a stick. I needed a helper for my garden, and when he told how fond he was of gardening, I got permission from the Mother Superior to employ him.'

I ignored the disgraceful slander contained in her second sentence. Something was puzzling me. 'He actually told you he was fond of gardening?' I asked in disbelief.

'Not exactly in those words,' she admitted, 'But you know the funny ways these people have of saying things. This pidgin English is so quaint. What he actually said was that he was good at forking, and I told him that it was my favourite hobby, too.'

I was speechless. The good Sister continued: 'He had nowhere to stay, so I fixed up the old potting shed behind the girls' dormitory for him. He seems to like it there.'

We looked back over the garden. My erstwhile employee was hacking away at the stony soil with an enthusiasm that would never have been suspected by we who had been privileged to work alongside him. I was the one to break the silence this time.

'Yes, Sister Mary,' I murmured. 'I bet he does.'

Chapter 12

MY OLD FRIEND LEOPARD

In the dry season it is as pretty a little stream as you are likely to find anywhere in the world. From its source near the blue of the sky it meanders its way downhill over bouldered scarps and through sylvan dells, gathering as it flows the little trickles of water that percolate down its sides even in the driest of dry seasons, resting here and there to form ever-larger pools for tiny fish to sport in, until finally it vanishes into anonymity midst the myriad streams and waterways that feed the mighty rainforests down below.

It has a modest start to life. It first sees the light of day high up among the crags bordering this vast forest, emerging shyly from its womb deep inside the granitic gneiss of the escarpment. Here it lingers for a moment, forming its first pool, a tiny pool in the shadow of the cliff, a pool of water so pure and cold and clear that, with the cool mists of morning still hanging heavy around you, you might be forgiven for imagining that you were quenching your thirst from a spring in the heart of the Canadian Rockies.

You have to take care as you follow it downstream. The slope is steep and the scree shifts easily and dangerously in a seiche of movement under your feet. One wrong step and you will find yourself tobogganing your way to the bottom with boulders of greater and greater size gathering momentum over and around you. There would be nothing to stop your descent; up here the vegetation is so sparse as to be virtually non-existent. There is nothing at all but stones and more stones.

Halfway down this steep gradient you stop. The mists are clearing and the morning sun is just beginning to peek over the edge of the escarpment. An eagle soars high over the top, far above you, like a fragment of charred paper drifting in the wind. Its harsh, lonely cry echoes hauntingly around the cliff walls even after it has vanished from your sight.

From where you sit among the rubble of stones you can see the rainforest below, an unbelievable, seemingly unbroken expanse of forest stretching to infinity. Down there, there is not so much as a breath of air to ripple the leaves anywhere throughout that vast sweep of greenery. It is silent and it is brooding and it is menacing.

It is waiting for you.

The scree comes to a dead stop when you reach the top of the foothills. Suddenly you are into low, scrubby montane forest, flat-topped bushes not much taller than European hawthorn trees. Here and there you can see the boles of stunted gboh trees rising above the scrub, and here you find the first sign of chimpanzee activity. The gboh trees – 'Parinari excelsa' to the purists – are in fruit and each tree has a carpet of fruit around it. The dusty-olive coloured fruit are a little like rough-skinned plums in appearance and they are good to eat. That the chimps have been here the night before is evident from the chewed remains scattered all about, and from the sleeping nests they have built in the flat tops of the scrub around you.

Walking is most pleasant hereabouts. The low, thick canopy forms an effective sunshade over the head and there is little or no undergrowth to snare the feet. Crumbly, purplish-red lumps of almost pure iron ore sprout out of the ground everywhere and hidden songsters fill the fresh clean air of morning with their sweet melodies.

You don't have to travel much further down the slope now before you see dramatic changes in the vegetation. The chimpanzee bush has vanished and suddenly you are on the fringe of the high forest. Statuesque azobé trees tower skyward wherever you look, sturdy of bole and straight as the pillars of the Parthenon. This is the ironwood of the Coast, an extremely hard and durable, dark-chocolate coloured timber that today lines many a Dutch sea wall and supports many a European railway line. The vivid rufous hue of the bark is quite startling in the half-light of the forest. Here also, the stream is a lot wider and a little deeper, but the water still filters gently through the smooth round stones on its way downhill.

Nearer to the bottom of the slope the character of the forest changes yet again. The ironwoods have gone now and the mahoganies have taken over. They are even more magnificent in stature and they dwarf every other living thing in the forest, their great spreading crowns locked far overhead in permanent embrace. The stream has changed too at this point, for sometime in the dim and distant past erosion has created a waterfall with a 12 foot drop and a deep, dark pool at the foot. Sometime, too, in the past a forest giant has fallen here, leaving a gap in the canopy that allows sunlight to filter through to sparkle on the tumbling waters.

This is where you stop, for there is no need to go any further. This is the place you have come to see. This is journey's end.

Nothing much had changed in the years that had passed since I had last been here. Liana-wreathed mahoganies still towered all around and clouds of multi-coloured butterflies hovered over the bright yellow flowers of a small *Ouratea* shrub growing out of the bank below me. Cicadas fricated endlessly in the thick undergrowth bordering both sides of the stream and the gentle waters still played their timeless lullaby as they spilled gracefully down the fall to the pool below. The sun still shone through the roof of the forest above me, on that grassy knoll across the stream as it had done in the old days.

But now only the bare yellow grass was there to reflect the light of the sun. That much had changed.

This was where I had first set eyes on him, lying on that grassy knoll on the opposite bank. This first meeting was, I think, as much of a surprise to him as it was to me. I had been here before on a number of occasions, and always for the same reason. Down there at the foot of the waterfall, if you were lucky and approached the bank with due caution, you would be able to watch sleek velvety otters playing, splashing and whistling to each other in the deep, dark waters. That was why I had come in the first place, to watch otters, and it was with a considerable jolt to the nervous system that I realized that, on this occasion, I had company.

He was lying on the short grass under the ancient sapele tree on the far bank, sunning himself, no more than 20 yards away from me. The old gold and the black rosettes of his coat gleamed in the evening sun, with the 50 shades of green that only Mother Africa can produce making a perfect backdrop to his splendour. He lay motionless, but his great amber eyes burned with a fire of their own as he watched me with a wary intentness from across the little stream, his body tensed and ready to vanish into the depths of the forest at my first careless movement.

He was a magnificent specimen of leopard and well he knew it. Although neither of us could have been aware of it then, over the next few months we were destined to see quite a lot of each other.

Although this was my first actual sighting of him, I had known since I arrived in the area several weeks previously that he was around. Indeed, by now I knew rather a lot about him. Locals who had seen him told me that he was very large and this I had had confirmed to me by the size of his prints. The fact that his diet seemed to consist mainly of larger animals such as waterbuck, bush-buck and wild pig indicated that he was in the prime of condition.

The local hunters were terrified of him. While all leopards are of a solitary disposition, this one was, by all accounts, the complete loner. He sought not the company of his own kind, whatever the sex. His range was extensive, and he guarded his territory jealously against any opportunist trying to grab a share of the rich pickings of game to be found in his area. Although he had been roaming around this neck of the woods for something like six years now, he had never been known to mate and he had never even been known to leave his territory in search of female company. The highly superstitious forest people considered him to be bewitched and kept well clear of him.

My next meeting with him was brief but explosive. I was standing on a little hill overlooking a swamp, plucking bunches of bush cherries from their slender stems. I leaned back against the tall, thin flange of a cotton tree, savouring the sharp, sweet-sour tang of the fruit, listening to the forest sounds in the heat of the day: the hollow WHOO-OOP-HOOP-HOOP-HOOP-HOOP of the wandering hoopoe, the churr of the ubiquitous cicadas, the wrangling of monkeys up in the verdant tops. I was revelling in it all, at peace with the world and myself in the hot wet air of this vast cathedral of everlasting twilight.

My reverie was shattered in startling fashion: a couple of hoarse barks from the troupe leader far above and the forest fell silent. I melted into the buttresses and waited. Seconds later I heard the frantic drumming of tiny hooves and a little duyker antelope shot past, eyes rolling in terror. Down the incline it scurried, to vanish from sight in the swamp. A couple of heartbeats later came the sound of a much heavier, rapidly moving body and Leopard hurtled past within a couple of yards of my refuge, his body a blur of black and gold, moving like a well-oiled machine, hot on the trail of his dinner. One colossal bound down the hill and he was gone like a streak into the tangle of thorns and lianas within the swamp.

We met often after that, mostly in less dramatic ways. I was returning home one evening from a pleasant fishing expedition, with a large catfish hanging from a piece of string in my hand. As I rounded a bend on the path I stopped abruptly. About 15 yards away he sat facing me, with a young bushpig at his feet. We stared at each other for a moment or two, then he picked up his trophy and turned away with a look almost of contempt, as though to say: 'Only a lousy catfish! Look what I've got!'

Mostly, though, we met in the vicinity of the waterfall. It was his private sunbathing spot, you see. We never did more than eye each other from our opposite banks and I kept a respectful distance from him. I never presumed upon our relationship by trying to get closer to him or overstaying my welcome. But I often came to see if he was 'in residence', and I invariably felt a twinge of disappointment when I found him absent.

I was away for some time, far away on the fringes of pygmy-land, involved in a tree survey of some sort. In those dense and rain-soaked forests, as yet untainted by the mechanics of man, elephant, gorilla and buffalo abounded. Even the shy bongo could be seen from time to time, though generally only as a dark wraith slipping away silently through the silver-barked obeche trees.

I should have been happy enough in this paradise of wildlife, but there was a certain restiveness about me, a sense of unfathomable depression that seemed to increase with the passing of the days. Nights were the worst. When the forest was bathed in moonlight and I lay on my stick-bed listening to the low murmuring of my survey crew around the camp fire, my thoughts would drift back inexorably to a sun-splashed glade by a waterfall in a distant forest . . .

The old village chief met me as I entered his compound, tired and filthy from a long trek back through countless swamps. I knew instantly from the gravity of his expression that he had bad news for me. 'The leopard has been shot,' he said without preamble. My body turned to stone. 'What happened?' I asked.

Sick at heart, I listened to the old familiar tale. A hunter, out in the forest with his musket loaded with scrap iron, had taken a pot shot at a shadowy figure in some dense undergrowth. The leopard sprang high in the air, spitting and snarling, then hobbled off into the depths of the forest, trailing a damaged foreleg.

For some days nothing at all had been seen or heard of him. Then, just as everyone had begun to think that they had seen the last of him, a goat was killed and eaten on the outskirts of the village. Then a dog. Then another goat.

With the remaining livestock now safely penned up, he had begun to harass the women and children in their excursions to the stream behind the village for water in the evenings. He had not yet harmed anyone, but it was obviously only a matter of time before hunger got the better of him.

'Where is the man who shot him?' I asked in cold fury. The old man waved his hand in vague dismissal of the question. 'The leopard was sacred,' he replied ambiguously, 'and the man was punished in accordance with tribal custom.'

I waited for him to continue, my mind in turmoil. 'I know how much the leopard meant to you,' continued the chief gently. 'But he has a strong juju, and none of my people will go near him. He cannot hunt now, and I am afraid for our children . . .' His voice trailed off into silence, but his meaning was becoming clearer by the minute.

'So what do you want me to do?' I asked. But even as I put the question, I knew with a sense of foreboding and inevitability what the answer would be. 'My friend,' he answered softly, 'we have only got old dane guns here, and you are the only one with a good gun. I want you to take the fear away from my people . . .'

Leopard had holed up somewhere inside the 'Place of Thorns'. This was a boulder-strewn plateau about half a mile from the village, an indescribably horrible tangle of spiny wild-lemon scrub, cactus, sawgrass, and every conceivable type of thorny, creeping vine. It was a sacred bush, so no one ever ventured into it. The place was reputedly alive with all manner of snakes, no doubt feeding regally on the colonies of rats and ground squirrels that lived in the holes and crevices among the rocks. The thought of having to track a wounded and highly irritated leopard in that appalling place filled me with dread and I did not need the second sight of my Hebridean forebears to know that this would prove to be one of the more nerve-wracking experiences of my life.

The following morning I entered the Place of Thorns, armed with a double-barrelled shotgun.

The Place of Thorns was even more forbidding than I expected. The clinging odour of mould, the sickly stench of decay, hung over it. Although it was riddled with tracks, most had been made by the smaller forest creatures such as pigs and duykers, which had been able to pass underneath the low ceiling of thorns. Most of my own time, therefore, was spent on all fours crawling along their tracks. The slightest touch on an overhead branch would bring down showers of stinging ants on top of me, and I was being torn and spiked all over. Once, only its loud, blood-curdling hiss warned me that I was about to put my hand on a colossal gaboon viper, that lazy, deadly denizen of the Coast. I was sweating copiously, and not only from the heat of the sun either.

Then suddenly I came across what I had been looking for – a well-worn path with leopard prints everywhere. Many were several days old, but some were quite fresh. The fresh ones in the damp, black soil between the rocks showed me the direction it had taken that morning and I decided to follow those, exercising extreme caution as I did so. It was without a shadow of a doubt my leopard, and it was resting often. It was badly hurt, and it would be very dangerous indeed.

I crept forward, stopping to listen every few yards, nerves a-jangle at the slightest sound. Visibility was very limited with the density of the scrub and I was conscious all the time that those great amber eyes could be watching my every move.

By noon I had had enough. I had lost his trail among the rocks and my body was on fire with the attentions of the ants and the thorns and the sawgrass. My nerves were in shreds and I was parched in the blazing heat. It was time to go home. I began to retrace my footsteps.

I stopped abruptly. Just yards from where I had about turned, there lay a pile of fresh leopard droppings! Droppings so fresh that they were steaming in the heat of the sun. I looked around quickly, gun cocked and my heart beating like a trip-hammer. But there was not a sound to be heard, not so much as a rustle in this wilderness of thorns.

His tracks were clearly visible and there was no doubt about what had happened. He had crept up to within a few yards of me, then just as silently and mysteriously he had turned and vanished in the scrub. Shaken and sorely puzzled, I hurried home, knowing that I would have to try again the following morning.

Next morning, very early, I sat on a steep rock outcrop overlooking the plateau. It was still dark, but on the very edge of the skirting of the trees silhouetted to the eastern horizon, the sky was fading from the deep dark velvet of night to a pale powder blue flecked with gold. Stars still flickered and pulsated in the sky, dimming as lighter shades of the purest jade spread over them. Dawn was approaching, and come daylight I hoped to have an eagle's eye view of any leopard movement down below me in the Place of Thorns.

By mid-morning, however, I knew it was hopeless. I had not seen so much as a cane rat move in the place. Indeed, I had seen nothing more exciting than a family of hornbills squabbling in the umbrella trees away below me in the valley. Of Leopard, there was no sign. I guessed that he would rest through the heat of the day unless disturbed. The whole tortuous stalking business of yesterday would have to be undertaken again. Today, though, there was to be no turning back. Today, I was determined to finish the job and end his suffering.

I approached the Place of Thorns from a different angle today and initially progress was a lot easier. The scrub was sparse, visibility was better, and I could stand upright. But then the scrub began to thicken and once again I was reduced to crawling. I was becoming more and more unhappy about this whole exercise. Although I had not yet seen any fresh signs, I could not shake off a strong sense of disquiet, a chilling feeling of being under constant surveillance. I stopped to rest and figure out my next move . . .

And there he was! It was as though he had materialized out of thin air. He was about five yards from me, lying on his stomach, unmoving except for a nervous little twitching of the tip of his tail. His eyes blazed like torches, unblinking, and his fangs were showing in a silent snarl. His shattered, suppurating left foreleg sprawled limply at an angle from his body, clouds of blue-flies hovering around it. He was desperately thin and his coat had the dullness of death.

I was paralysed, unable to move a finger as we stared at each other for what seemed an eternity.

He was the first to move. He turned and moved stiffly away from me, those marvellously fluid movements of yore gone now, moving like an arthritic old man, his foreleg dangling sadly and uselessly below him. He turned into the thickets and was gone forever from my sight.

He was never seen or heard of again.

The village people maintained, of course, that what I had seen was a ghost, that the leopard had always been a ghost, that he had now returned to his spiritual home where the sun always shone and the game was abundant.

But I knew better. Leopard had been flesh and blood, and only the death of things made of flesh and blood could bring the vultures to this place in the heart of the rainforest. When those grisly undertakers appeared, dark and sinister, over the Place of Thorns, I knew that the end had come.

And I was glad of it. For which of us likes to see suffering in those who have been close to us?

*   *   *

You sit by the waterfall, listening to the pepperbird's warble from its perch on the branch overhanging the knoll where Leopard used to rest. Silver-and-blue tigerfish flicker and swirl in the pool below, snatching at the beetles and grasshoppers that fall from the overhead branches. The sky is an azure blue but your own mood is dark and sombre.

Even after all this time, the manner of his passing affects you. But even more than that, there was your own lack of courage in the final analysis. Neither to end his agony nor to save your own life could you have pointed that gun at him.

But suddenly, like the first hint of dawn at the end of a long and sleepless night, another thought comes to you: twice, while you were stalking him through that awful scrub, he had had the chance to kill you, but twice he had turned away at the last moment.

Why?

Was it because he too felt that this would be just no way to treat an old friend?

Chapter 13
THE TOURACOS OF PUTU

Even during its periods of relative stability, Liberia would not have ranked highly on the list of 'musts' in any holiday brochure. Graham Greene travelled through it from west to east in the early 1930s and recorded his experiences in *Journey Without Maps*, and Gérard Périot (*Night of Tall Trees*) travelled through the central part during the 1950s. Neither had much that was complimentary to say about the country.

Today, as the 20th century draws to a close, political instability is such that only the very foolish would attempt to travel through the Liberian hinterland, given the unlikely eventuality that they would be able to secure the necessary authorization to do so from their embassies in the first place. I spent rather longer in Liberia than either Greene or Périot, though at a much later date. During the 1970s I travelled extensively through many of its more remote forests. One of the more interesting of those was the vast area of semi-deciduous forest surrounding the Putu Range in the north-central part of the country.

Though probably not more than a couple of thousand feet high, the crags of Putu look spectacular on one's first sight of them, jutting upward as they do with such startling suddenness out of the surrounding mantle of green. To see them at their best you have to see them with the sun upon them, for their heavy quartz deposits make them glitter like silver against the verdancy of the forest. In my day, before the inevitable logger moved in to remove the best of the trees, the forests around the crags contained all the rich panoply of tree species that one had come to associate with the more unspoiled parts of the White Man's Grave, and the diversity of wildlife species was quite remarkable.

Most of the usual commercially acceptable species could be found in abundance in the Putu forests. On the drier slopes to the south and east of the range one would come across large pockets of obeche. Botanists call this most sought-after, white-timbered tree *Triplochiton scleroxylon*, and it was just as spectacular in appearance as in name. This was a real forest colossus, and it was a singularly beautiful tree. Like the crags that spawned it, its bark sparkled silvery-grey in the sunlight, and it was very gregarious: where you found one, you were liable to find hundreds. At the height of each dry season they shed their leaves, reminding one compellingly of the grandeur of the Canadian fall as the big, maple-shaped leaves tumbled slowly and gracefully to the ground.

I remember the area around the tiny village of Geeblo, south of the main Tchien to Cape Palmas road, being particularly scenic at this time of the year. The huge boles with their massive, distorted branches outlined in stark nudity against the eggshell blue of the sky 200 feet above you, stood amidst a six-inch deep carpet of newly fallen leaves. The ground everywhere was suddenly transformed from its normal anonymous brown pastel to every known hue of gold, red, green and bronze.

Among the forests of Putu could also be found the usual mixture of mahoganies and other commercially acceptable species. But, as always, it was often the less well-known species that attracted my attention most, and, as was usually the case, these were the ones that did not immediately catch the eye as you walked through the forest. On the contrary, it sometimes seemed that nature had so designed them that they would be forever hidden in the crowd. The kanda tree was one. *Beilschmiedia mannii*, to give it its scientific name, was a most inconspicuous tree, never – by African rainforest standards – very big; at best, it might have aspired to a height of 90 feet and it was skinny and sinuous. It was of little interest to the commercial logger, but it was of enormous interest to the natives of Putu. Its timber, leaves and bark were most beautifully fragrant, and the flowers gave a delicious tang to cooked rice. Never a really common tree anywhere in Africa, it was probably more common in the Putu area than anywhere else I had been.

The coula tree was very common hereabouts. Chimpanzees loved its fruit. About the size of European walnuts and vaguely similar, the nuts were full of oil and much esteemed by the people of the forest. I was very fond of them myself. During the fruiting season, when the small, branchy parent trees would invariably be hanging heavy with the hard-shelled nuts, the village women would gather them by the basketful for sale and barter in their markets.

Another one of the smaller species common around the Putu hills was the afina tree, or *Strombosia glaucescens*. This was a skinny, knobbly-stemmed understorey tree whose curiously scaly bark left it looking as though it was clad in an army camouflage coat of ochre and green mottling. The bark and roots were much used in juju medicine, being pounded to a paste in a mortar and applied to the afflicted parts of those suffering from deformities of the feet and hands. The extremely hard timber of this species was used for poles in house building and for mortar pestles. During the 1930s it was even exported to England, where, for a brief period, it became popular as a flooring material in dance halls. The timber was not only attractively streaked with buff and purple hues, but it had the remarkable property of wearing smoothly like marble under constant foot traffic, not splintering as other timbers tended to do. Perhaps fortunately, the fact that it was rarely to be found in other than pole sizes precluded its use for export in anything but rare and tiny parcels.

Movingui – or 'monkey-can't-climb', to give it its local name – was another attractive and quite common tree of the Putu hills. Called *Distemonanthus benthamianus* by the scientific establishment, it could be quite tall, sometimes even topping 100 feet in height. Its height was often exaggerated by its rather skinny and sinuous bole and by its lightly branched crown of feathery, light green leaves. The loggers made occasional use of its yellowish-green timber. Its bark, however, was what made it really stand out in the forest. It was of a most vivid rufous-brown colour, often flaking off in papery strips to show an inner bark of the brightest green. Once seen, this tree was hard to forget. It got its local name from the fact that the very fine bark flakes made the bole surface slippery and impossible for even the monkeys to climb.

Two very large species of tree to be found commonly around the Putu area were decidedly not popular with the commercial logger. As timber trees, they were not even popular with the locals. They were simply far too hard. *Parinari excelsa* grew everywhere in Liberia. It was especially common around Putu, where it formed large, gregarious stands. It could grow to over 150 feet in height, and it was a very handsome tree indeed. Its timber was chock-a-block with silica, and any sawmiller trying to run a parcel of logs of this species through his saws was seeking financial suicide. Its fruit, called 'rough-skin-plums' by the indigenes, were much sought after by elephants. More like small, rough-skinned mangoes in appearance, they were also eaten with relish by the local people, and during the fruiting season the ground beneath the trees would be absolutely covered with them. I have often eaten them when hungry, but I did not care for them much; I found them too dry and mealy to my taste.

Manilkara obovata was also common around the Putu area. It was a huge tree and so hard of timber that it actually looked hard from the outside. It was generally avoided by the locals, although they used branches of fallen trees for fuel as it made the best firewood of all. Its masses of little yellow flowers opened at dawn, filling the morning air with their sweet scent. At noon there would be a steady rain of falling petals from the treetops, and their heavy, honey-fragrance would be all around you as you tramped them underfoot on your travels.

'Out of the strong came forth sweetness,' as a much better writer than I once put it.

One tree found in abundance in the forests of Putu was not only popular with the European timber people. It also had, for much of this century, been even better known to the general public than the mahoganies. It had a name that was familiar to every little boy who had ever read adventure tales about African voodoos in the years between the two great wars. This was the sasswood tree, sometimes known as the 'ordeal tree', and known to the world of science as *Erythrophleum ivorense*.

The sasswood was a strange tree. Without knowing either its name or the legends about it, you instinctively knew that there was something not quite right about it the moment you saw it for the first time. It could be a large tree, often up to 150 feet in height and four feet in diameter, with, generally, a crooked bole and a heavily branched, rather gloomy crown of the darkest bottle green. Its bark was very rough and scaly and muddy brown.

This description, written several thousand miles away and an aeon removed from the arcanum that surrounded the old Africa that I knew, seems bland today as I read it. It is, indeed, a description that could have been applied to quite a number of rainforest trees. But this one was somehow different. I remember vividly how, standing before my first one on my own in the heart of the forest, just gazing at it, the surrounding trees and undergrowth suddenly became still and the hairs on the back of my neck began to tingle. The whole aspect of the tree is one of sinister gloom, and even its timber – popular all over Europe to this day for its excellence in parquet flooring – had a cold, brassy glow to it that seemed oddly like the surreal glow that emanates from the ancient bronzes of Benin.

The sasswood tree has always been renowned in fact and fiction for the use of its poison in the so-called 'trial by ordeal'. The bark, when cut or bruised, exudes a thickly copious, dark-red liquid. This contains a very virulent poisonous alkaloid which, in the old days, was much used in settling grudges, and in native court procedures to test the guilt or innocence of the accused. The accused was made to drink a bowl of the poison in mixture with palm wine. If he or she died, guilt was presumed. Recovery was regarded as proof of innocence. The trick, I was told by a witch doctor, was to gulp the mixture down rapidly so that the stomach, rejecting it, would vomit it up immediately. Those who were confident of their innocence would adopt this tactic, I was further informed, while the guilty who expected imminent death, would sip it slowly, thus giving the poison time to be absorbed into the system.

This was the theory, but like all theories it was by no means infallible. Poison from an old tree was nearly always fatal however quickly or slowly the victim drank it. To this day, there is no known remedy.

I have a poignant, lasting memory connected with the sasswood tree. On the outskirts of the pretty little village of Geeblo on the edge of the Putu Range there is a grave marked by a concrete slab. It covers the spot where the beautiful Bahee lies. She was poisoned by sasswood. Leaves from the towering obeches surrounding the village flutter gently over the site during the dry months of the harmattan, forming a glorious, multi-hued carpet over her grave. It is a fitting place to rest, for she, too, loved the obeche as much as she feared the sasswood.

I have always had a tendency to think of certain tree species in human terms, in a masculine and feminine sense. It is the old 'silver-birch-is-a-dainty-lady' syndrome, of course, and it is a piece of nonsensical romanticism that has no place whatsoever in the metabolism of a hardened forester. But there you are. It is present in me, and there is no point in denying it.

Naga (*Brachystegia* species) is a great, thick-armed brute of a tree that totally dominates the forest around it, to the extent that little else is permitted to grow in its awesome shadow. It would be the Mike Tyson of my tree world any time. Although it can be very tall – often growing to 200 feet in height – it never quite seems to be as tall as that, so great is its diameter. Even at that height, its eight-feet-plus diameter bole makes it look rather squat and burly. Beautifully cylindrical, it is devoid of branches for nearly all of its length before suddenly sprouting a few mighty limbs out at right angles to form an umbrella of smaller branches and grey-green foliage all around it. Orchids grow profusely on its crown, and ropes of liana hang all the way from the topmost parts of it to the floor of the forest.

There is little undergrowth in pure naga forest. This is because the leaves take so long to decompose, and they form a black leathery carpet around the tree. This appears to have a stultifying effect on regeneration. Wild pigs and elephants occasionally rest up in naga forests on hot afternoons, but generally animals stay clear of them, for the simple reason that there is little to eat in their permanent shadow.

But naga forests were most pleasant places in which to camp, particularly during the harmattan months. The first cool mists of November to come drifting down from the north seemed to be the cue for all kinds of activity to commence in the treetops. What seemed like a minor war would erupt as the naga seed pods burst open with pistol-shot cracks, releasing their hard little seeds to drop in a steady pitter-patter of sound to the ground below. Orioles gave occasional flashes of their golden glory in the gloom, and the hollow call of the wandering hoopoe could be heard everywhere. Flocks of grey parrots wheeled tirelessly overhead, and the skies were endlessly blue following the rains.

Naga was common around Putu. It was here that I had my first real encounter with the most extraordinary bird it has ever been my good fortune to see. I had seen touracos from time to time throughout the rainforests of Africa, but never in such abundance as in the Putu area. For reasons that remain something of a mystery to me, this strange bird seemed to have a particular predilection towards the naga trees of Putu. Here, they performed their quaint rituals high up in the tall trees, bowing their heads to each other like gaudily-painted geishas during a night out on the town, and here they mated and nested and reared their odd little chicks.

In fact, everything about this bird was odd. In flight, it looked the most prehistoric of creatures as it flipped and flopped laboriously from tree to tree, reminding one irresistibly of stick-and-canvas pterodactyls sailing over forbidding landscapes on a Hollywood backlot.

There are many different species of touraco. Some are even savannah dwellers, but the forest touracos are the colourful ones. They vary in size from about that of a rook to a peacock. They eat fruit — mostly figs — and leaves, buds and flowers of a variety of tree species. Essentially arboreal, they are most often seen when loping along the great limbs of the forest gallery like demented Groucho Marxes in pursuit of God knows what. They are the least enthusiastic of flyers, preferring instead to glide from tree to tree wherever possible. Despite their secretive nature, they are very social with each other and they are very noisy, communicating in loud choruses of barks and grunts. One is aware of the presence of touracos in a patch of forest long before one enters it.

Their heads are crested and often tipped with red or white. Mostly, their bills are stubby and small. But it was for their plumage that the touracos first raised the eyes of the world of science. On first sight, it appears loose and rather fluffy, but closer inspection shows it to have an almost metallic lustre, with the most incredible shades of blues and violets and greens seen anywhere in the bird world. One of the things that makes this bird so special to ornithologists is the fact that the green coloration in its feathers is produced by turacoverdin, the only green pigment known to occur in birds. Equally interesting is the fact that the dazzling red of their wing patches is created by turacin, a copper-bearing pigment that is also unique among birds and is easily removed from their feathers by soaking in a chemical solution.

The biggest of all the touracos was the one named as the 'great blue touraco'. If the others were secretive, I found nothing shy about this bird. On account of its size and coloration, it was called 'peacock' by the hunters of Putu – a name that they probably got from white hunters of long ago. Unlike the other touracos, the great blue had no red feathers on its wings, but its plumage was the deepest, richest blue I have ever seen on any living creature. The great blue touracos were even noisier than the others. They made an incredible din, and when one started up it was the signal for every other great blue touraco in the vicinity to join in the chorus – a jarring KOW-KOW-KOW-KOW-KORUK-KORUK-KORUK-KORUK racket that would clatter out over the trees and rattle among the crags of Putu as the birds made their long glide from the naga tops to their feeding grounds among the fig and umbrella trees far below.

I regret to state that I have, from time to time, eaten various species of touraco. I have never done so with any degree of enthusiasm. Without exception, I have found their flesh to be black, stringy, bitter and rather horrible, and this is one African delicacy that I do not expect to find featuring regularly on the menus of the better European hotels.

Touracos, I am told on good authority, make fine aviary birds. I am sure that is so, and any system that guarantees their survival must be lauded. I have never seen them in a cage, aviary or zoo, and I rather hope that I never shall. Touracos, to my mind, belong only where I remember them best, and that is in the great rainforests of Africa.

Increasingly, as I grow older, there are times — especially when the cold English rain comes slanting in from the North Sea and over the bare lands of winter — that my thoughts drift back over the years. Then I find I am listening once more to the cracking of hard woody pods on green-capped, ghostly giants, and the still heat of the African day is with me and the air is full of the patter of seed falling to earth around me. It is at times such as these that I hear, yet again, the haunting cries of those strange, primordial birds as they scuttle along on their mysterious ways among the orchids where the roof of the forest meets the blue of the sky in far-off lands.

And I see, too, those gold and red obeche leaves drifting gently on the warm zephyrs over a grassy mound under the fragrant lemon bushes outside a tiny village in the middle of nowhere when the world was young and I was younger.

God's heaven must be made of dreams such as those.

Chapter 14

TO SKIN A GORILLA

'*Ex Africa semper aliquid novi*', remarked a gentleman called Gaius Plinius Secundus, apropos of nothing at all, during a conversational hiatus at a Roman soirée back in the days when Anno Domini was just clocking in her first century. Somewhat loosely translated, this could be taken to mean that the Africa of that era was full of surprises.

Pliny the Elder, as he was better known to his friends, had said a mouthful. He knew what he was talking about. Even back in those days the great sea-faring nations of the Mediterranean were involved in quite a lot of toing and froing between Europe and the hot green shores of Africa, and they had had more than their share of surprises. In fact, long before Pliny's time, some even more adventurous souls than they had made the occasional foray far into Africa's interior. One of the earliest recorded expeditions, more than 2,000 years before the birth of Christ, had been made by one Herkhuf, a governor of one of Egypt's most southerly provinces. He followed the Nile deep into the heart of Africa, returning with a shipload of ivory, frankincense and ebony. Also – so the story goes – being the consummate show-off that he was, he just had to bring back with him something new and extra special with which to entertain his friends. He had, he felt, every reason to feel pleased with his coup. Deep in the hold of his ship, securely shackled and incandescent with rage, he had one tiny, stark naked pygmy.

The pygmy excepted, there was nothing very new about

Herkhuf's cargo. Ever since the era of the caveman, ivory and pelts have been in demand. Just as primitive man started the slave trade, so did he instigate the trade in animal products. It is just that nowadays there is a lot more of the human race than there used to be, and its demands are that much greater. And its weapons of destruction are that much more sophisticated. The elephant had some chance against the spear and the flintlock, but he had none whatsoever against the range and velocity of the modern weapon.

But Herkhuf's pygmy was significant. This was blatant one-upmanship at its most outrageous, and it is this factor more than any other, the all-consuming desire to have something better, rarer, more exotic and more expensive than one's neighbour, that has led to the near-total extinction of Africa' s great and ancient wild heritage.

*   *   *

'Have you ever skinned a gorilla?' asked the Frenchman. I looked up startled. 'What the hell would I want to skin a gorilla for?' I demanded.

The old man gave the butt of his shotgun one last wipe with the cloth, stuck a cartridge in the end of each barrel to foil the attentions of mudwasps, and propped it back in its regular corner of the living room. Then he came back to join me on the verandah.

'Around the Coast in the old days,' he replied enigmatically, 'you were neither a hunter nor a proper naturalist unless you could skin a gorilla.' He paused to tamp down the tobacco in his pipe, then he fumbled in his pocket for a box of matches. It was, I thought ruefully, going to be another long night of story telling.

We were sitting in his mud-block bungalow on the banks of the N'Zo River, in western Ivory Coast. Earlier that day we had been out shooting guinea fowl in the savannah scrub behind his house, and we were now trying, quite unsuccessfully, to cool off over a cold beer or two on his verandah. It was a sweltering hot night at the beginning of the rains. Rhino beetles droned around us in graceless, lumbering flight, like grossly overladen transport planes, caroming sightlessly into the wall, their heavily armoured bodies making dull clunking sounds wherever they made contact, and hordes of suicidal moths fluttered endlessly against the pressure lantern on the stand behind us, the grey-white powder from their wings suspended in the still air around the hissing light. The old man sucked contentedly at his pipe, then picked up his beer and continued:

He had left France many years ago as a callow youth of some 18 summers to work for an uncle who ran a trading store in French Equatorial Africa, several countries to the east of where we now sat. It had seemed like a great adventure at the time, and for the first couple of years it had been just that. However, selling tins of sardines and bolts of cheap cloth to missionaries and market mammies soon began to pall on a lad who had been used to the freedom of outdoor life in rural Brittany. The acquisition of an ancient musket gave him the escape hatch he needed and, on the pretext of trying to supplement their spartan diet with antelope and green pigeon, he began to spend more and more time away from the store in the company of black hunters, learning from them the art of trapping and snaring, and generally frightening the wits out of the local population of monkeys with the thunderous explosions from his bundook.

Professional white hunters occasionally called at the store to buy provisions, most of them poachers who had found themselves *personae non gratae* across in their regular stamping grounds in Uganda and Tanganyika, and had drifted into the unfamiliar jungles of the west to keep their shooting eye in until the furore they had left behind them had died down. None of them stayed too long; not only was it more difficult to spot game in the rainforests than in their own great plains, but they seemed to be more prone to the fevers and sicknesses that could beset even the hardiest in the swamp forests of the interior. In addition, there was the near-insoluble problem of getting their booty out to the coastal markets.

One of those who stayed long enough to get to know the young Pierre was an old Belgian ivory hunter. He took a shine to the boy and was impressed by his enthusiasm and desire to know all that he could about the techniques of hunting. Under the old Belgian's tuition, he had developed into a good and careful shot, and he had begun to learn the nuances of the bushcraft that was to become his life. It had come as no great surprise to his uncle when, shortly after his twenty-first birthday, Pierre and the old Belgian had left the store and headed through the great forests of Ubangi-Shari to make their fortunes in ivory.

They were after a special kind of ivory. The forest elephant was fairly common hereabouts, and this was their target. Smaller than the elephant of the eastern plains – it rarely exceeded seven feet in height at the shoulder – the forest elephant also had much smaller tusks. But its tusks were much sought after as the ivory was esteemed above all by collectors, being of the purest white, harder and closer grained than the yellow ivory of its larger cousin. However, it was much more difficult to locate, favouring as it did the swampier regions of the rainforest, and it was of a much more suspicious and evil-tempered disposition, particularly when it sensed that man was on its trail.

But the old man and the boy made a good team. They knew that they had to hurry, since the dry season in central Africa lasted only a fraction of the time that it did on the Coast. They worked hard and put their combined bush expertise to good use, so that by the onset of the rains they had as much ivory as their porters could carry. They struck eastward through the forest towards the Oubangui River, hoping to find river transport to take them down-stream with their tusks to Léopoldville, near the mouth of the mighty Congo River.

Good fortune did not exactly favour them. One of their porters went down with yellow fever and the virus spread rapidly, wiping out half of them in short order. The remainder dumped their loads and vanished one night, leaving Pierre and the Belgian to find their way out of the forest as best they might. They wrapped their tusks in swamp leaves and buried them, marking the tree under which they had planted their cache for future reference. Then they started the long trek home.

It was to be the old Belgian's last hunt. Somewhere in the midst of all these endless swamps and forests, he rather recklessly left his tent early one morning to attend a call of nature without observing the elementary precaution of taking his rifle with him. A vengeful elephant caught him, trousers around his ankles, in what is probably the most undignified posture of all, and young Pierre buried what was left of him shortly afterwards.

The boy never returned for the tusks. He had lost his taste for elephants and everything connected with them. In any case, it was doubtful if he would ever have found them again in the vastness of the Ubangi-Shari jungle. He had, in addition, other matters to occupy his mind after he found his way back to his uncle's store. One of the many things the Belgian had taught him was the art of skinning and curing, and this knowledge he was able to put to good use soon after his return. His uncle had for years been boosting his meagre income by the sale of parrots, baby chimpanzees and other wildlife to traders and itinerant zoo collectors. Now he had received an intriguing enquiry from an American source for a dozen gorilla skins. This he passed on to his nephew. Young Pierre knew the forests at the juncture of the Sanagha and the Ngoko rivers, not much more than a day's march away, like the back of his hand, and he knew them to be full of gorilla. This was the break he had been waiting for. He packed his gear and prepared for his first trip into the bush as a fully fledged hunter.

The youngster's knowledge of the area and his natural rapport with the forest people now stood him in good stead. Teams of pygmies armed with nets and spears were set to work to round up the great apes and in no time at all he had all the skins he needed. The scenes of gory bloodletting during this appalling slaughter seemed not to have fazed him at all, and when, following his triumphant return, orders came pouring in for exotic pelts of every kind, he knew that he had found his forte . . .

'But how,' I interjected, 'does one skin a gorilla?'

'Simple!' replied the old man. 'You skin it just as you would skin a rabbit; it just takes a bit longer to do. It takes three men to do the job properly, and it takes them around three hours to skin a full-grown male gorilla. Then it takes a further four hours to 'thin' the skin; that is to say, to remove all traces of fat and so on sticking to the inside of the skin. After that, the skin is staked out and dried in the shade for three more days – too rapid drying would shrink it – and it is then preserved with brine.'

'Do you still hunt for skins?' I asked.

'Not any more,' he said wistfully. 'It was hard work, and I'm too old now for the long treks involved.' He puffed at his pipe, gazing out into the darkness. 'Besides,' he added, 'the trade in gorilla skins has long gone. Although, mind you, I'm told that the demand for leopard and golden cat skins is greater today than ever it's been.'

'But gorilla skins!' I exclaimed incredulously. 'What in God's name did they want with those?'

'My young friend,' replied the old man mysteriously, 'there is no accounting for human vanity!'

The trade in skins and ivory has long been a monument to human vanity. Before the coming of the white man to Africa, chiefs adorned themselves with skins of guereza and diana monkey and draped strings of leopard teeth around their necks. Witch doctors collected the tusks of giant forest hog and the whiskers of the male leopard for their jiggery-pokery, and pelts of one kind or another could be found adorning the huts of most able-bodied bush Africans. But all of these items were simply a welcome by-product of the creature that the hunter had killed only for food in the first place. Nothing was ever wasted. Every single part of the animal had its use in the everyday life of the African of the forest.

The coming of the white man soon changed that. He was not interested in the meat; he was interested only in the by-product. He introduced the safari and the high-tech weaponry to the simple native. And he introduced greed and vanity.

What had been a relatively peaceful co-existence between hunter and hunted now became all-out war, with the odds very much stacked in the white hunter's favour. Trophies were hung on walls in distant lands. Pelts were laid on marbled floors and draped around elegant concubines. Elephant and hippo feet became umbrella stands in baronial halls. It was only a matter of time before the mystic Orient joined in the scramble to see who could be the first to decimate forever the wild life of Africa – their weird obsession with aphrodisiacs all but put paid to such marvellous behemoths as the rhinoceros of the eastern plains.

It was slaughter on a grand scale, and neither the white colonials of the past nor the black politicians of the future did anything much to stop it.

Many years after my meeting with the old gorilla hunter, I was working my way slowly along the bank of a rocky, fast-flowing river in the Liberian hinterland. The fishing had been poor, but I did not really care. After a month of being stuck in an office down on the coast, it was a relief to get out in the fresh air of morning. It was a glorious day. A gentle breeze ruffled the feathery branches of the ubiquitous ho trees crowding each side of the river, and in the dappled sunshine under a sprawling kiasoso tree a cluster of multi-coloured butterflies hovered over a pile of its rotting, yellow fruit.

I climbed up the small incline on the bend of the river, marvelling at the idiosyncrasies of Nature that she should make such a lovely and delicate creature as a butterfly prefer rotting vegetation and excrement to flowers. At the top of the knoll, I came to an abrupt halt. I was looking straight down on the back of a magnificent, fully grown leopard.

The sun gleamed on his coat as he lapped thirstily at the water's edge. Although only a few yards separated us he was, as yet, unaware of my presence. Then the wind shifted every so slightly and suddenly his great eyes were blazing up at me, scorching me with their intensity, the only movement of his body being the habitual leopard twitching of the end of his long tail.

We stared at each other for what seemed a millennium. Then he coughed loudly and hoarsely, an explosive sound that was half growl, half clearing of the throat. I stood stock still, my fishing rod over my shoulder, and he turned his head away from me and sauntered off into the shadows, vanishing from my sight within the thickets without so much as a backward glance.

Not long after this incident, for reasons that need not detain us here, I found myself on a brief visit to the self-proclaimed 'sunshine state' of California, USA. During this visit I was dragooned into attending one of those ghastly functions that people with far too much time and money to spend seem to idolize – the cocktail party. The venue for this particular shindig was one of the more prestigious hotels in Los Angeles, and it seemed to my jaundiced gaze that most of high society from Los Angeles and beyond were crowded into that vast function room. You could almost smell the wealth. I took the first glass of liquor proffered to me and – as always when in situations not to my liking – I sought shelter in the nearest clump of bush. A huge rubber plant in a relatively quiet corner attracted my attention and I made for it.

I studied the scene before me. The coruscating chandeliers above were no more hurtful to my aged eyes than the bejewelled magnificence of the ladies holding court on the floor. They simply shimmered and glittered and sparkled with the slightest movement of their bodies, while their courtiers hovered anxiously around them lest some voracious male should spirit them away to even more opulent surroundings. Suddenly, I remembered a verse from the works of Tennyson:

> Man is the hunter;
> Woman is his game:
> The sleek and shining creatures of the chase,
> We hunt them for the beauty of their skins.

I looked at the walls behind them. They were adorned with the heads and pelts of what had once been some of the world's more impressive creatures – tiger, polar and grizzly bear, elk, musk ox, plus a variety of African big game – while a huge moose head gazed down lugubriously upon the gathering from above the door. Situated dead centre among the kudus and things was an intimidating portrait of Theodore Roosevelt. I was reflecting that, since in all probability this old hunter had accounted for a high proportion of the casualties scattered around him, it would have been more appropriate had his own head been nailed to the wall among the rest, when I realised that I had company. An expensive-looking young lady had sneaked up from downwind of me and was addressing me:

'I hear you're from Africa?'

'Yes,' I replied cautiously.

'And you live in the jungle?'

'Well . . . er . . . yes. I suppose you could say that . . .'

Given the sort of company we appeared to be in, I suppose there was a certain inevitability in her next question:

'Have you seen any big cats out there?'

My reply that the only 'big cat' to be found in my particular part of Africa was the leopard did nothing much to quench her thirst for information about 'the jungle', so, in an endeavour to get rid of her, I told her the story of my recent encounter beside the Liberian river. With hindsight, I suppose I should have anticipated her reaction. She heard me out, round-eyed, then she sighed: 'Gee, didn't you wish you had a gun?'

I stared, aghast, at this appalling woman standing before me. Then I asked her with some asperity: 'What on earth would I have wanted to shoot it for? It was doing me no harm.' With the devastating logic of her kind, she replied: 'But they make such beautiful coats . . .'

On the tip of my tongue was the ancient cliché that, in my opinion, the coat always looked better on the animal, but I didn't bother uttering it. I would have been wasting my breath. Here was a young lady who had never known the glory of a leopard basking in morning sunshine on the bank of a tropical river, and whose only thought when I tried to describe its beauty and its majesty to her was a desire to have it shot and stripped of its skin so that she could wear it.

This, truly, was the law of the jungle. The white man's jungle.

Yet it had all begun so innocently. Primordial man had killed a sloth to feed his family. Just one lousy, ordinary sloth, as he had done so many times before. This time, though, instead of chucking the pelt on the bed or the floor to join all the other skins in the cave, he made what was to be the biggest mistake in his life. He told his wife it would look pretty on her. She put it on, and it looked so good that she couldn't resist swanking to her neighbour in the next cave about it.

The next thing they knew, Her Next Door was wearing a tiger skin, and we all know what happened after that.

Today, *Homo sapiens* is a lot smarter than he was a few decades ago. Not for him the rigours of the chase and the discomforts of bush, veldt and tundra. He stays at home shooting tame pheasants while the suckers, the black poachers, do the dirty work for him out there in the boondocks. He can buy his tusks and his rhino horns and his leopard teeth through the black market, and as for all those other little legal necessities for momma – well, he can still take care of those via the furs department of the nearest big store. And because he has the money and is prepared to pay enough to feed a starving nation for one fur coat, the slaughter will continue in one way or another until there is nothing left to kill.

That caveman had a lot to answer for. One-upmanship started with him. So did wimpishness. How much better for the world today would it have been had he applied his club to his spouse rather than to that unfortunate tiger.

Chapter 15
HIBISCUS LOVE

Nothing more illustrated the difference between the black and the white cultures of the Coast than their approach to marriage. The black man was polygamous by nature and inclination, while the white 'Coaster' was, in general, monogamous. The very thought of having a cluster of women managing his domestic affairs would have been enough to make the toughest of Old Coasters reach for his nerve tonic, while – out in the bush, at least – the black man's first ambition on the day he acquired Wife Number One was to save up the wherewithal to be able to afford Wife Number Two. And so on, practically *ad infinitum*.

Polygamy suited the African of the bush. It was something of a status symbol; the more wives a man had, the more successful he was seen to be. A man with one wife was deemed to be poor, but a man with several was obviously a man of some substance. Indeed, in some tribes it was the custom for a wealthy chief to farm them out from time to time to the poorer of his tribesmen, which gives a whole new meaning to the term 'donations to the under-privileged'. The chap with the moolah not only got the prettiest girls around (a sad fact of life also in much more enlightened societies), but – more importantly for the bush African – he got the hardest workers and the best cooks. In addition, he hogged the market in those considered most likely to be fertile, and nothing in life was more important to him than that.

Usually, the wives would be billeted together in one of the larger huts in the village, with the senior wife in charge of the whole ménage. Her authority over them was absolute. She acted as counsellor to them and as confidante to her husband, passing on to him any snippets of gossip she might have heard from the other wives or from the village market. All of them got on remarkably well together and jealousies only surfaced when he appeared to be favouring one wife more than the others.

There was usually plenty of competition to become Wife Number Something of a man of means. There were undeniable perks to be acquired through becoming one of the team. Each wife would be allotted her own plot of ground on her husband's farm, to grow and sell for herself whatever produce she wanted. There was the additional bonus that a wealthy man could afford plenty of wives, and the more he had, the more time each wife had for doing her own thing, for her own share of the daily domestic chores would be that much reduced.

To those unused to the ways of Africa back then, it might have seemed to be a relationship no more meaningful than that of the barnyard rooster with his flock of hens, and I have some doubts as to whether such estimable organizations as the women's liberation movement would have thought much of the whole deal. I am no anthropologist, and I am certainly not an apologist for an archaic system that denied the right of woman to choose her own destiny. But it seemed to me to be a system that worked remarkably well for that particular era and for that particular part of the world. I don't remember ever meeting one black wife who seemed unhappy, and they were always ready to stop what they were doing to crack a joke with you whenever you met them on your travels, even when they happened to be total strangers to you. And how often do you find that these days in our more liberated societies?

But there was no doubt that man was the real winner in the marital stakes. He had it down to a fine art. The more wives he was able to gather around him, the less work he had to do on his farm himself. In fact, the less of anything he had to do. Finally, he had achieved what had been his goal in life all along, which was to have nothing left to do with his time but to eat, copulate and sleep, and be waited on hand and foot during every waking hour. It was the ultimate masculine dream, whatever colour of skin the man happened to have. The difference was that it had to remain nothing but a dream for the white man.

'How very different,' remarked some wit once upon a time, 'to the love life of our own dear Queen Victoria.' One could never have imagined the colonial lady as Number Anything Wife to some fat old chief in the back of beyond. Apart from anything else, it would have been beyond her physical capabilities, and not just from a sexual point of view, either. The work load alone would have killed her, used as she was to invigorating temperate zone climes that made physical labour a joy rather than a burden.

Boredom, though, — particularly boredom through having too little to do — begets mischief, and boredom figured highly in the metabolism of many colonial wives. Somehow, the ones living on isolated stations far out in the hinterland seemed to cope with it much better, perhaps because they forced themselves to do something, whether it was pottering around their compounds chivvying garden boys, rearing chickens or showing their cooks how to make preserves.

It was usually in the larger European communities that the trouble started. Endless coffee mornings and days of idling around the swimming pools at expatriate clubs while their men were at work were ideal environments for cooking up ideas to relieve the monotony. Some wives went further than most, and one little group achieved brief fame through the dottiness of their anti-boredom wheeze.

The town in which they lived had better remain anonymous, as had the names of the participants themselves. Those who are alive today would not thank me for being indiscreet, for they are undoubtedly sweet little old grandmothers by now, every single one of them, running church bazaars or whatever in the land of their birth for the overseas missions, and few people wish to be reminded of their youthful indiscretions when they are basking in the warmth of respectability that comes with age.

They were six in number, and they had organized a competition which, for want of a better name, they had called 'the Venery League'. It was a cute little idea, in which the eventual league champion would be the one from their six who would prove successful in seducing the greatest number of men over a given period of time, blacks and sailors excluded. I do not know whether any trophy was awarded to the winner, but I believe that the points system was quite complicated, extra points being awarded for fixtures played away from home. If my memory serves me correctly, one point only was awarded for the conquest of lowly, sex-crazed timber men straight out of the forest; a sliding scale of four to six points for the various grades of trading store managers; seven to nine points for the different types of colonial civil servants, and ten points for virgins and ambassadorial staff. A bonus was on offer for the virtually impossible bedding of such as Baptist missionaries and visiting cardinals but, so far as I was aware, this bonus was never collected.

Almost inevitably, the participants became known as 'the Easy Six'. Anything masculine, white, and appearing to be reasonably human who ventured out of the bush and into the town wherein they had their lair did so in the certain knowledge that he was facing the greatest possible threat to his virtue. Not all, alas, were deterred by this fact.

This, mark you, had nothing whatsoever to do with prostitution. The Easy Six were above that sort of thing. They did it only for the fun of it. They were all married to singularly docile husbands who spent far more time in the European Club than in their own homes, and they were all husbands for whom the bar and the billiard room presented far less challenge than the hurly-burly of the marital bed. If they ever heard whispers about the Venery League, they pretended not to know. It was easier that way. Besides, they could console themselves with the knowledge that, in the end, their wives were almost certain to remain with them. Very few marriages ever broke up as a direct result of Coast liaisons. Love among the hibiscus blossoms – even adulterous love – was almost an accepted fact of life for many of those who sought their fortunes under the aphrodisiac skies of the White Man's Grave.

Occasionally a husband would have his fling, too, but rarely openly and absolutely never while his nearest and dearest was on the Coast. When he did stray, it was always during his wife's frequent and seemingly interminable vacations back to her homeland. But very rarely would he start messing about with someone else's wife; the risks were just too great. The thought of being caught and of having a vengeful wife hot-footing it out to the Coast with murder in her heart was just too awful to contemplate.

But, as the children grew up and the need for them to receive the best possible education became more and more pressing, the partings inevitably became longer and longer. The husband feeling the pinch of such lengthy partings was expected to grin and bear it. In practice, either he got rid of his surplus energy on the squash and tennis courts when the long day's toil was over, or he drank himself into an alcoholic stupor before bedtime.

Only the most foolhardy would have dared take unto himself a mistress. Such libertinage, while considered almost de rigueur in the French colonies, would have been regarded as being highly improper by the British administration, especially if the lady in question happened to be an indigène. Being suspected of 'going native' was the surest way of finding yourself on the first boat home.

The Morleys – I shall call them that, though this was not their real name – had never had to face this dilemma. Those best acquainted with them knew that the sanctity of this particular union could never be disrupted by sexual desire for each other, far less for anyone without the constraints of their marital vows. They were just too upper-crust. An archetypal colonial from the crown of his ridiculous topee to the soles of his calfskin mosquito boots, George Morley had been posted to our delightful little town in the interior many years previously as bank manager and he had no wish ever to leave it. Here, he was king.

More correctly, here he was prince consort. His wife was the undisputed monarch. An unabashed snob who dominated every social function for miles around, Penelope Morley terrified everyone, including her husband.

Her absences from the Coast were mercifully frequent and prolonged. One would have thought that her husband would have been glad to see the back of her, but, in truth, he looked a lost and lonely figure without her. He spent a lot more time in the expatriate club than usual on those occasions, drinking steadily and telling interminable stories about banking to anyone within earshot. Most felt sorry for him, but rarely sorry enough to invite him to dinner. It always seemed such a waste of an evening to have to entertain such a thundering bore.

I suppose that none of us would have become privy to the last chapter of the Morley saga had not Ben the Bar confided in me. Ben was the senior steward at the club, and he was liked and respected by everyone. Everyone, that is, except the Morleys. During his spell as chairman of the club some years previously, George Morley had been involved in a campaign to have Ben sacked for some trifling misdemeanour. Ben had survived, but one of his numerous brothers – also employed as a barman – had not. Although he was smart enough to realise that Penelope had been the instigator of the campaign, Ben was a Tiv, and Tivs never forget a grievance. Years after everyone else had forgotten the incident, Ben's habitual joviality would evaporate noticeably whenever the Morleys entered the club premises . . .

I had been away from the area for some time, and on my return I called at the club. Ben the Bar looked inordinately pleased with life, so I asked him if he would like to share his good news.

'The Morleys have gone!' he informed me.

'Gone!' I exclaimed, startled. 'Gone where?'

'Home to England. For good!' he replied smugly.

It was early in the evening and I was, as yet, the only customer. I bought him a beer and settled down to listen to his story.

Penelope's last act before departing on vacation had been to have one of her more violent contretemps with their two domestic staff, her long-suffering cook and houseboy. Tired of her tyranny, the servants had fled the moment her car had left the compound. When Morley returned from the metropolis after seeing his wife off, it had been to an empty house, and he had hired as houseboy the first lad to come to him with a decent reference.

His choice of cook was less conventional. George Morley had succumbed at last to the temptations of the Coast.

Comfort, for that was her name, took charge of the house. She was an excellent cook and she produced wild and exotic dishes from her kitchen that Penelope had probably never even heard of. She was a pretty little thing, too, and she taught him wild and exotic things in bed that Penelope had most certainly never heard of.

There was an effervescence about her that seemed to brighten the darkest corners of his gloomy old house. She and the new houseboy had hit it off instantly. They sang as they attended their domestic chores and the sound of their singing followed Morley down the verandah steps each morning. As he drove sedately through the town to work it was a sad fact that his thoughts were invariably focused less upon the banking problems of the forthcoming day than upon the happy turbulence that had so engaged him in the Morley four-poster during much of the preceding night. George Morley, in other words, had never know such contentment in his life.

The bombshell that was to blow his elysium apart caught him quite unprepared. It came via a cable from his head office on the coast. Penelope had arrived and was on her way by hired car to see him. Someone had blown the gaff on him.

George Morley had never been regarded as a man of action. Even to his few admirers, words such as 'phlegm' and 'inertia' came most readily to mind when describing him. Not, it has to be recorded, in this instance. Now, he was transmogrified. He left his office like a ferreted rabbit. Seconds later he was streaking for home with that frantic urgency best exhibited by erring husbands the world over when attempting to extricate themselves from similarly unpleasant predicaments.

He made it by a whisker. Comfort and her accoutrements had just been shovelled out the back door when Penelope arrived at the front, travel-stained and bristling with suspicion. She informed him she had received an anonymous letter to the effect that he had been misbehaving and she had decided to pay him an unscheduled visit to see for herself.

It was a tricky moment, but Morley had covered his tracks well. Not a trace of his mistress remained and, as he had kept her existence a secret from the outside world, none could betray him. A modest sweetener had secured the houseboy's silence and the crisis was averted.

Then Penelope had one of her predictable rows with the houseboy. It was, as usual, about something trivial – the incorrect folding of napkins or some such nonsense – but it could hardly have happened at a less opportune moment: the touring British ambassador and his lady were among the many interested spectators. As her tantrum reached its crescendo the houseboy stalked out, pausing at the door to fire the fatal broadside: 'Old woman, you are no bloody gentleman. This was a greatly happiness home when the black Mrs Morley was here.'

'And that,' concluded Ben, 'is why the Morleys have now retired to Europe after long and faithful service on the Coast.'

I gazed pensively at him. 'I wonder who could have sent that letter to Mrs Morley?'

Ben's expression was that of a man quite untroubled by his conscience. 'The mills of God grind slowly, sir,' he intoned softly.

'Ben,' I said, 'you're a cunning, vindictive old rascal.'

'Yes sir,' he replied imperturbably. 'That's what my younger brother tells me. He says that it runs in the family.'

'Your brother?'

'Yes, sir. Mr Morley's houseboy.'

The silence that followed was broken only by the steady CHUNK . . . CHUNK . . . CHUNK . . . of the ceiling fan. Ben's eyes were dreamy as he lifted his beer mug. 'My little sister keeps emphasising the value of strong family bonds. You must meet her, sir. She is a good cook and she is very pretty. She would be good for you.'

I sipped my drink slowly. 'Yes, Ben,' I said, 'I'm sure she would.'

* * *

The Coast was made for bachelors. There was never any doubt in my mind about that. As the open prairies of the Old West were made for the free-spirited cowboy, so was life in the White Man's Grave only really suited to the single man, and only to a certain, very special type of bachelor at that. Especially, it was bachelor's paradise for the dreaded and much maligned 'trades people'. While the stiff-upper-lip formality of the colonial administrator was such that his main source of enjoyment was the occasional Embassy party, the rougher diamonds working for the smaller business concerns really knew how to let their hair down. There were plenty who didn't make it through their first tour, of course, and only a very small proportion of them returned for a second helping. But those that did were hooked for life. Mother Africa had trapped them finally and irrevocably in her black silken web.

None could adequately explain why they stayed on, year after year. When pressed as to why they should want to spend the best years of their lives in a malarial, snake-infested, sweltering wilderness, they would reply, rather self-consciously and defensively, that they were only doing it for the money.

That, of course, only touched on the truth. They also did it for the excitement and the sort of freedom that life in West Africa offered them in these days. Especially the freedom. They worked hard, but they also played hard. Timber men from all over Europe and iron miners from the likes of Saskatoon and Kamloops played harder than most. Once in a blue moon, they would up stakes and head for town. And, when these lads hit town, they hit it very hard. To the casual observer, it must have seemed at times as though these wild men from the bush, making whoopee after months of monk-like deprivation, were trying to kill themselves with alcohol and sheer bodily abuse in their few short days on the town.

Stuffy colonial-type institutions welcomed them not. Perhaps because of this, these same institutions were often the first port of call for the thirsty revellers before they dispersed to seek out the bars in the shadier parts of town. They were impossible to remove from the premises. Polite entreaties would usually be greeted with lively derision and threats to have them forcibly evicted would be greeted with even livelier derision. Nervous hotel managers and club secretaries tended, therefore, to take the easy way out: they would find a quieter part of their premises in which to entertain their more regular guests and members while they sat it out until the unwanted guests had had their fill and shoved off to pastures new. Until that blessed moment came, the visitors would entertain them right regally, rattling the rafters with old Coast ditties:

> First I was posted to Lagos;
> Keen as a ram to begin,
> So I purchased a young Ibo virgin
> For the price of a bottle of gin.
>
> Ugly and oily and smelly,
> Like a she-devil she were;
> Oh I got such a fright
> On that very first night —
> But I learned about women from her ...

They were eccentrics, one and all, and they came from all walks of life. Old Battle of Britain pilots and Grenadier Guards officers caroused amicably in the company of former Luftwaffe pilots and members of Rommel's Panzer Korps, their former enmities forgotten, all of them out here on the Coast desperately seeking what little adventure there was left in the world now that their war had ended. There was a great camaraderie within their ranks. They rarely fought with each other, but they would participate with much enthusiasm when one of their drinking companions became embroiled with some outsider or other.

Life was never dull around them. I remember a burly Geordie ex-paratrooper who was scared stiff of moths and hurled beer bottles at them whenever they fluttered into his house at night. His aim could be erratic when he had had a few drinks and guests frequently had to take evasive action as shards of glass and showers of beer sprayed the room and those sitting in it. A favourite party trick of his was to throw new-laid eggs at the electric fan. Ladies put on their oldest clothes when invited to dinner at his house.

For a year or two I was friendly with a cowboy from Idaho, who now worked for a logging company in Liberia. He had suddenly quit his job of rounding up strays for the Carnation Milk Ranches back home because, as he so eloquently explained to me: 'Ah jest got plain tired of comin' in at nights with ma ass frozen to the saddle.' Now, his cowboy hat, his spurs and his well-scuffed chaps hung as much-admired mementos behind the door of his house in this, one of the most unpleasantly hot countries in the world. I would often drop in to have a chat and a beer with him. He was a fascinating raconteur, and his tales of life as a cowboy out on the range enthralled me. With a beer or two inside him, he would recite the Carnation Milk anthem:

> 'Carnation Milk is the best in the land;
> Here ah sets with a can in mah hand;
> No tits to pull, no hay to pitch -
> Jest punch a hole in the sonuvabitch.'

Nights on the town in this cowboy's company often developed into a competition to see who could spend the most money fastest. Perhaps because of my Caledonian background, it was usually a competition which I had no trouble in losing.

I have equally vivid memories of François, a most easy-going Roquefort fisherman who worked for a shipping company on the Coast. He had a black girlfriend nicknamed 'the Monkey Woman' because she had a pet monkey that she insisted on being allowed to accompany her wherever she happened to be. François called it 'Laval', and no doubt he had good reasons for doing so. It was a mangy, evil-looking brute with long, yellow fangs and breath like a vulture's. The Monkey Woman was no oil painting herself but I liked her, as did just about everyone who met her. She was full of fun. The monkey, she informed me once, was insanely jealous of François and it would sit sullenly on the rail at the foot of their bed, glaring at them night after night while François had his wicked French way with her.

While neither of the lovers seemed to have been in any way disconcerted by the ape's baleful voyeurism, theirs was obviously a relationship fraught with peril. It ended rather sadly one night when François was comfortably ensconced in what I believe is known as the primate position with his mistress. Laval flew at him like a tiger from its perch on the bedrail, biting a large chunk out of his left buttock. It was, François told me later, the fastest withdrawal since the Italians met Montgomery in the desert. François shot the monkey stone dead as, sensing it had gone a bridge too far, it headed off across the compound in the moonlight at speed. The Monkey Women left in high dudgeon, never to be seen again.

On one never-to-be-forgotten occasion I helped to fish the scion of one of Britain's more eminent peers from the filth of an open sewer that ran round the perimeter wall of a rather lowly African brothel. He had plunged into it in the darkness while in hot pursuit of one of that establishment's star performers, with whom he had suddenly fallen in love. I regretted almost instantly the mad impulse that had driven me to help him out of it; he stank to high heaven and he was plastered from head to foot with ordure of such glutinous viscosity that the proprietrix of the bordel had no hesitation in closing the door firmly in his face when he attempted to go back inside. He was the picture of dejection as he stood there in the moonlight, faecal matter sticking to his moustache and sewage oozing slowly from his Savile Row suit. 'What,' he bleated plaintively, 'would my father say if he heard that his son had been refused entry to a common African fornicatorium?'

Such disparate nationalities, such incredibly varied back-grounds. But they were workers, all of them. They worked their socks off, uncomplainingly and for months on end without a break, in conditions that would have the trade union leaders of today calling for nationwide strikes. When they came out of the bush, their benders were the stuff of legend. They drank and they caroused and they wenched until, their money gone and their baser desires assuaged for the nonce, they returned quietly and soberly to the stations from whence they had issued forth with such raucous clamour just a few short days before. And civilized people breathed again.

Africa will not see their like again. Today, they would be jailed and deported. The winds of change that began to stir the leaves on that great continent in the 1960s blew with hurricane force through the White Man's Grave. In the space of a few brief years every country along that coastline had achieved independence and the old white characters had gone. This new Africa had no time for the expatriate eccentric. A different sort of white was required now, one who would not stand out in a crowd, one who would be sensible and conventional and docile, one who would be happy to accept the fact that his place in this new order would be a very humble one indeed. There would, of necessity, be a sort of Orwellian greyness about this new generation of white, a greyness that would be the greatest possible contrast to the colour of the old brigade.

They had to go, these old-timers. Like the ones who made the Old West, they were a law unto themselves. They integrated with no one and they took orders from no one, white or black, unless they liked the person handing out the orders. Like the characters of the Old West, their time had been right for being there. But their time had come and their time had gone now, and to those of us who had lived through it all, it had seemed to have lasted no time at all.

But, by God, they had most surely left their mark on the place.

Chapter 16

THE DRUNKEN CHIMP

The great crowned eagle sailed high over the forest, soaring round and round in ever-widening arcs, coasting along with majestic ease on the soft warm billows of air that flowed gently down from the arid dunes of the Sahara far to the north. It was a seemingly aimless circling, just the drifting of a harmless silhouette against a powder blue sky, wings stiffly outstretched like a toy plane, with only an occasional twitch of its rudder to give any indication to the watchers below that the cruising shadow had heart and lungs and beak and talons and that it was not entirely indifferent as to its final destination.

To the casual observer it might have been a serene and almost somnolent sight, but the little colony of mona monkeys watching intently from the tree canopy far below could not be classified as such. They were well aware that the eagle was not coasting around up there simply because it liked the scenery, and that the slightest lapse on their part, any momentary relaxation of their caution, would have this, the greatest of all African winged predators, tumbling out of the sky in a flash to bury talons deep into fur, flesh and sinew.

The harsh KEE-KEE-KEE call of the eagle faded as the wheeling silhouette became smaller and smaller before finally vanishing from sight. The forest relaxed. The black and red weaver birds in the swamp palms resumed their ceaseless bickering and the bullfrogs their deep-throated croaking in the dark, oily waters. From somewhere inside a clump of slender abura trees growing on the edge of the swamp, the distinctive fluting call of an oriole rang loud and clear once more throughout the sunlit glade.

Ignoring the cautionary bark of the elderly troupe leader hidden in the tree canopy, a flighty young female monkey scampered along the branch on which she had been perched, silent and impatient, during the eagle's reconnaissance. She raced to the end the slender branch which bent under her weight and, without hesitation, launched herself into space, arms and legs outstretched to clutch the thickly coiled liana spiralling from the roof of the forest to the ground below. Down this she sprinted, reaching the forest floor in seconds. Here she paused for a brief moment to hurl a stream of yattering defiance up at the troupe leader, before bounding off on all fours along the edge of the swamp.

Under the untidy, sprawling branches of a massive fig tree she paused and sat on her haunches, peering with bright-eyed curiosity at the antics of the weavers as they slung their fragile-looking nests precariously from the underside of the palm fronds overhanging the stagnant waters. She yawned and scratched her ribs, then scanned the fruit scattered all around her. She picked up one of the fat green figs and studied it thoughtfully.

In the dense tangle of foliage halfway up the fig tree, where he had been concealed since his mate had begun her aerial distractions, the mighty raptor had watched and waited for just such a moment. He opened his wings slowly and silently.

The little mona monkey was raising the soft sweet fruit to her mouth when the eagle fell like a thunderbolt upon her . . .

I had witnessed the little drama unfolding from the cover of some scrub on the other side of the swamp. I watched now as the eagle flapped heavily out through the branches with his victim while the monkeys fled in noisy panic through the treetops. His mate had appeared out of nowhere and was now circling low overhead, calling to him, her duties as a decoy successfully accomplished.

Through the thin cloth of my bush shirt I could feel the trembling of the tiny pygmy squirrel inside my breast pocket. He had been sitting on my shoulder nibbling at a peanut when the eagle's shadow had flickered over the clearing and he had instantly vanished into this, his own private sanctuary. There he would remain, curled up in a tight little ball, nose and eyes buried in his bushy tail, shutting out the horrors of the world outside until I could assure him that it was safe to emerge again.

As I picked my way carefully around the edge of the swamp, I pondered on the instinctive fear that many creatures seemed to have for winged predators. Not even the creeping, cold-eyed snake can fill them with the same quivering dread. But they often lose their fear completely when their *bête noire* is on an equal footing with them. I have watched monkeys endlessly tormenting a perched eagle, ganging up on it, two approaching it from the front and pretending to snatch at its legs with their long spidery arms, holding its attention while another approached it from the rear to pluck at its tail feathers midst shrieks of hilarity from the primates and squawks of outraged fury from their victim. But the moment the eagle took wing to escape them, their mischievous bravado turned to abject, frantic flight. Perhaps this was deep-rooted in all creatures, a legacy from the dawn of time when ferocious bat-winged pterosaurs roamed the early skies in their ceaseless quest for prey?

Clumps of grey-green fur marked the spot at the foot of the fig-tree where the mona monkey had met her untimely end. I moved inland from the swamp a little, carefully checking over the ground under the trees through which the monkeys had taken flight. At such moments of extreme panic, little ones had been known to fall to the ground and indeed it was only the week before that I had picked up a badly injured youngster at this very spot. I patrolled the ground painstakingly, tacking back and forth slowly, checking into every hole and corner before, satisfied at last, I set off for home.

Inside my pocket the little squirrel stirred slightly, chittering uneasily as he buried his tiny face deeper into the soft fur of his tail.

The parrot greeted me with a piercing wolf whistle as soon as I entered the bungalow. I eyed her meditatively. For someone who had always been so much against the idea of keeping wild creatures in captivity, I seemed to have acquired an incredible collection of them over the years. At the moment I only had Squirrel and Parrot, plus a young chimpanzee answering to the equally unimaginative soubriquet of Charlie. At one time or another, though, I had had a succession of antelopes, guenons, civets, mongooses, otters, hyraces, and so on, most of them brought to me by hunters who had shot or trapped the parents for food. By parting with a few judicious pennies here and there, I could save yet another orphan from following its mother into the communal cooking pot.

But one major problem with keeping the young of any species for any length of time was that they became totally dependent on the surrogate parent, making their return to the wild virtually impossible. Furthermore, there was my nomadic way of life. Animals needed the security of a permanent home, and they needed a lot of care and attention. My work kept me away from home for long periods of time and this meant that any livestock accumulated by me in my travels had to be taken care of by someone other than myself. This burden inevitably fell upon the increasingly bowed shoulders of Peter, my major-domo cum general-factotum.

Few of the creatures that came into his care lasted the course. This was not due to lack of attention on his part. Neither he nor I knew much about the care and maintenance of such very young things. Some died of dysentery and some died of constipation. Antelopes seemed to favour a peculiar form of glaucoma as a way of getting out of this world. Others just plain died. After each death I would vow to myself that never again would I be conned into becoming foster father to the first distressed animal I encountered. But whenever I came across a shivering mite with large appealing eyes lying beside the lifeless hulk of its parent, I would sigh with resignation and reach into my pocket for the adoption fee.

Squirrel's mother had met her end in a trap intended for much larger game than she. I happened to be with the hunter who had set it at the time he was doing his daily inspection of his trap line, otherwise the orphan, clinging to his dead mother's fur, would simply have been abandoned as being too small to bother about. I made the hunter's day by rewarding him with the magnificent sum of one penny for the tiny creature. At that time Squirrel was not much bigger than the penny itself. Now, a full year later, he was fully grown at about three inches long, with a luxuriant dark red, two-inch long tail. He was the only member of my little family allowed to come on my travels with me and he spent much of his time eating and grooming himself on my shoulder, or just simply curled up asleep in my pocket. He was terrified of practically everything on earth and he thought I was God.

'Bugger off!' intoned a dark brown voice from the shadows in the corner of the room. Parrot was letting me know in her own inimitable way that she wanted more attention from me. I walked across to where she sat perched on the back of a chair and scratched her head, thinking of our first meeting over a year ago. She was very lucky to be alive. Of all the creatures that had passed through my hands, Parrot had seemed the most hopeless case of all.

Life had kicked off with a thunderous wallop for her. I heard the crash of a falling tree as I was on my way home from bush one day. Some workers had felled a heavy-crowned afara tree on the edge of the river I was about to cross. One of them came over for me in his canoe and I watched for a time as they beavered away with their axes, hewing off the branches clustered around the top of the great trunk. I was about to proceed on my way when I heard one of the axemen calling to me from within the tangle of branches. I clambered over the huge limbs to see what the excitement was all about.

There were lying on the ground, two of them, stark naked and stone dead. They were about the size of common house sparrows, barely recognizable as being the young parrots that they undoubtedly were. They had not been long hatched, and they did not possess a single feather of note between them. They had been pitched out of the nest hole on impact and killed instantly. I fished about inside the hole and extracted another chick. This one, remarkably, was still alive, undoubtedly saved by the fact that it had somehow managed to remain inside the tree. For a few seconds Parrot's fate hung in the balance as I contemplated putting the poor little thing out of her misery. Then I wrapped her up in a handkerchief, placed her carefully in the pocket of my bush jacket, and headed for home.

I had not the slightest hope of keeping her alive. For a start, I hadn't a clue as to what to give her. Fully grown parrots, I knew, were very fond of the fruit of the oil palm, common in this part of Africa, but Parrot was obviously far too small to be able to tackle that. It was Peter who hit upon the bright idea of starting her off with a mixture of palm oil and coconut water.

There was nothing wrong with the idea. Getting the stuff into her was the problem. Several attempts with a teaspoon had only resulted in most of the goo getting plastered all over her. We eyed the miserable looking little scrap, now slimy and bright orange in colour from the palm oil. Then Peter suggested helpfully: 'What we need is one of those rubber things that white women use for feeding their babies.' I looked sourly at the man. 'Where the hell am I going to get a baby's dummy around this place?' I asked with some asperity. 'The nearest white women are 100 miles away, and they are Catholic nuns!'

We solved the problem finally by adapting a fountain pen filler for the purpose. This was before the era of the ballpoint pen and, like many others on the Coast (where the humidity was so high that things perished easily) I carried a good stock of spare fillers for my pen. This little gadget worked admirably.

Parrot never looked back. She was constantly hungry and it soon became obvious that neither Peter nor I were going to have the time to give her all the attention she required. However, Peter's nephew – a little chap of about eight years of age who answered to the curious name of Paraffin Oil – undertook the chore of feeding her for sixpence a week and he stuck to his task commendably until Parrot was completely weaned.

Within the year she had grown into a very handsome bird indeed, garbed in shades of the glossiest grey, from slate-grey on her back to silvery-grey on her head and front. Her tail, a vivid scarlet, was her pride and joy and she spent much time preening it.

She rapidly became a splendid mimic, imitating to perfection such bird sounds as the lovely morning warble of the pepperbird and – less melodiously – the racket of hornbills quarrelling in the mango trees outside.

There were times when I could have wished for less expertise in the art of mimicry from her. I still have clear memories of one occasion when I was away from home for an extended period. Peter had gone to his Biafran homeland with his wife and, rather naively, I had let myself be persuaded into allowing some very playful Irish missionaries to look after Parrot for a couple of months. She eventually returned to me with a vocabulary that would have done justice to a Clydeside riveter. It transpired that the good Fathers had spent every waking hour teaching her words and phrases that, one hopes, were not on their curriculum during their seminary training.

Parrot must have been a receptive pupil; some 10 years later she still had an adequate command of most of the expletives. Her timing was invariably immaculate, her diction of a startling clarity and her *bon mots* produced at moments when they were sure to have the most profound effect upon her audience. They added a new dimension to those drowsy English Sundays in her later life, lending a piquant sense of the unexpected to the still summer air when gaggles of elderly ladies of genteel disposition would drop in for tea and crumpets after church. Fortunately for my own already tattered reputation, her profanities were delivered in the distinctive Cork and Galway brogues of her tutors, which at least gave me some semblance of an alibi when Parrot was in full song.

Parrot never forgot an injury, intended or otherwise. She developed a deep and abiding distrust of Paraffin Oil, the lad who had to a great extent been instrumental in helping her into this world. The explanation was quite simple – Paraffin Oil was the one who gave her her periodic bath. Parrot was quite fond of water, but she objected to having others dowse her in the stuff.

Charlie the chimp was another for whom she had a deep and unrelenting antipathy. She hated him with every fibre of her being. In this case she had much more valid grounds for her dislike. He had humiliated her grievously, and this no lady of spirit will accept from the opposite sex. I was witness to it. A succession of piercing shrieks from the kitchen one day brought me rushing into the house, convinced that she was in the process of being murdered. I found Charlie sitting on the kitchen table, Parrot held in his left hand in a grip of steel. On the table beside him lay a small collection of bright red tail feathers. His rugged features were wreathed in the most beauteous smile of sheer contentment as he slowly and methodically plucked the few remaining feathers from her bald and wincing bottom.

She never forgave him.

Lady Luck had also favoured Charlie. A missionary doing his rounds among the little villages of the interior had come across a hunter heading for home with the body of a female chimpanzee slung across his shoulders. In the leather satchel swinging by his side he had her baby, whimpering like a child, with a single shotgun pellet embedded in the flesh of his upper arm. Charlie had been hitching a ride with his mother when the hunter had shot her and he had been fortunate in that he had stopped only one pellet. As I was living not too far away at the time, the missionary had brought his charge to me and, between us, we had managed to extract the pellet. The wound healed rapidly, and in no time at all Charlie had established himself as the household favourite.

He had also fast established himself as the household pest. So long as someone was around to keep an eye on him, he was no trouble at all, but the moment he was out of sight, he was up to his ears in mischief. It was for this reason that we built him his own quarters at the foot of the compound. It was fenced in, but he had a spacious run attached to his maisonette, a run which encompassed part of an ancient mango tree to provide him with shade, fruit and exercise.

He had many visitors, for he loved attention and the company of human beings, and he was an unashamed show-off. He had a trust in the human race that was certainly not shared by me and he would eat anything handed to him. Children were a particular hazard. On one occasion he accepted a few slabs of some singularly viscous American chewing gum from some visiting children and it took me the best part of an afternoon to unglue his jaws from the horrid stuff.

Charlie had developed an early and disturbing fondness for the demon alcohol. For this I blamed Peter. I returned home unexpectedly one day to find the two of them sitting on chairs in the kitchen, looking like a couple of bishops in the middle of a profound ecclesiastical debate. Each had a jug of palm wine clenched in his fist. Peter made the rather feeble excuse that drinking palm wine on one's own contravened his tribal laws. He added – rather acidly, I felt – that, in any case, Charlie, even in his cups, was better company than some people he knew. He may have had a point, but after that I ensured that the drinks were locked up when I was away from home.

It was Charlie's taste for the booze that introduced him to one of the hazards of socialising with humans – the hangover. A party of young Americans had descended on my little bungalow one Sunday and had accepted my invitation to stay for lunch. Charlie was an instant hit with them and they had no difficulty in prevailing upon me to allow him to join the party. After warning them not to let him get too close to their drinks, I repaired to the kitchen to help Peter with the food. One of the visitors had put a Scottish dance-music record on the gramophone and from the kitchen I could hear the whoops and bellows of the revellers as they pounded their beer tankards on their side tables in time to the music. When the racket turned to shouts of hilarity, I went through to investigate.

The cynosure of all eyes was Charlie. He was holding centre-stage, as drunk as a lord. (I discovered very much later that some idiot had given him a tumblerful of my best cognac, which he had quaffed instantly and with bibulous relish, without so much as batting an eyelid.) A guest had fitted him out with one of her children's tartan skirts and he was performing a sort of simian Highland fling for them. Up and down, up and down, pranced this hirsute, kilted drunk, hooting excitedly, falling down and rolling over and over on the floor in his attempts to regain his footing. Finally he hoisted himself upright in the wobbly, uncoordinated way of drunks the world over, cackling foolishly and immoderately all the while at the sheer exhilarating joy of it all. Never had Mr Jimmy Shand's Accordion Band performed to a more appreciative gathering, and never had an ape enjoyed life more than on that gloriously bacchic Sunday morning.

Alas, as the poet Burns, (who had much experience in these matters) once wrote: 'There's death in the cup – so beware!' The following morning Charlie had reason to ponder upon those cautionary words. He looked like hell. He sat under his mango tree, head held in both hands, rocking back and forth on his heels, uttering loud, heart-rendering moans. I entered his run and spoke to him, giving him my condolences, dispensing the infuriating, moralizing advice that those who have imbibed sensibly the night before never fail to impart upon those lesser mortals who have been all too free with John Barleycorn. He glared up at me through puffy, bloodshot eyes, quite obviously unable to believe that anyone could talk such rubbish to him in this, his hour of greatest travail. I placed my hand on his fevered brow and he bit me savagely.

The groans of a very sick chimp echoed around the compound as I hurried to my house to staunch the flow of blood from my injured wrist. My injured feelings took a lot longer to heal.

Charlie was with me for a further seven years. While it could not be claimed that this one drunken spree made him teetotal for life, it certainly made him more selective in his choice of tipple. The very sight of a cognac bottle was enough to send him scurrying down the hill to his own quarters, and the only person he every really trusted with drink again was Peter.

Parrot has retired to a farmhouse in darkest Essex. She is 40 years old, but looks and acts like a maiden half her age. She is completely infatuated with her guardian, my brother-in-law, who contributes little to her welfare, but she cannot stand his wife, who does everything for her. She displays amorously to him while sitting on his knee at nights, but my sister's daily routine of putting food and water in the cage threaten her fingers with amputation from Parrot's ferocious beak.

Parrot is jealous. She has set her sights on my brother-in-law, and no mere wife is going to stand in her way. She has been too long in the company of humans and she mimics their ways, good and bad.

Parrot has adapted well. Charlie is no longer around to violate her and she has long ago sorted out the local cats. The chinking of chaffinches and the hooting of owls have replaced the clamour of the weavers and the tinkling of the waxbills in her repertoire. She has learned to whistle obscure Aberdonian ballads and she imitates perfectly my sister's raucous squawk of 'PHONE' to call her husband in from the farmyard when the telephone rings.

Inevitably, being at heart nothing but a very common parrot, the more vulgar the sound, the more apt she is to latch onto it. An elderly countryman who dropped in now and then attracted her immediate attention. His habit of smoking a disgusting old pipe in front of the fire fascinated her, and she was intrigued by his repulsive habit of hawking great gobs of phlegm from the soles of his boots to launch them like guided missiles into the heart of the fire. Not only has Parrot perfected the gruesome sounds made by the old man in his efforts to haul his cargo of sputum up to the launching pad; she has also copied his physical contortions in the doing of it. Most stomach-churning of all is her mimicry of the finale – the splat and sizzle as the foul clot hits the red-hot embers at the back of the fire.

It is Parrot's party piece, her personal Grand Guignol, and it is the one that seems to give her the most ghoulish satisfaction. It is an exhibition guaranteed to clear the room in ten seconds flat.

It is many years since Parrot left Africa for good. But even now, when she has been consigned to the patio on glorious summer evenings to enjoy the balmy breezes and to hurl insults at the doves roosting in the cedars at the foot of the lawn, the fleeting shadow of an overhead kestrel will send her to the bottom of the cage in trembling panic as the ghosts of ancient Africa come rushing back through space to haunt her.

It is said that those who have dined with Mother Africa will forever yearn to return to her shores. Perhaps, as Parrot sits dozing with shoulders hunched and eyes half-closed on winter nights when the wind is whining in the chimney and the yellow flames curl round the hissing oaken logs, she dreams of far-off lands? Dreams of joining the flights of chattering, whistling, red-tailed parrots as they swift-wing their way over mist-wreathed, brooding forests? Does she, like me, dream of sunlit skies and graceful, swaying palms and towering mahoganies and village mammies with shining, ebony faces singing their way to market with headpans piled high with exotic produce?

And if she does, then what of it? We old timers are entitled to our dreams. We are both, after all, from a vanishing race. We are both Old Coasters. And we have both been privileged guests at Mother Africa's bounteous table.

Chapter 17

THE HARLOTS OF MUNDONI

The rains were drawing to an end at long last and the newly white-washed walls of the Forest Department bungalow shimmered and sparkled in the glare of the afternoon sun. The Oni River, heavily swollen and reddish-brown in colour from its cargo of latosol, surged in sullen haste past the foot of the compound on its way to the Bight of Benin, picking up en route much the same jumble of flotsam that might be found at this time of the year in any one of the rivers charging south to the Niger Delta. It was nature's great annual spring-clean of her equatorial forest belt, and the rivers were her garbage collectors.

Not that Forest Officer John Murgatroyd was in any mood to philosophize on the grandeur of it all as he sat boiling slowly in the heat of his verandah. On the contrary, he was moodily sipping a glass of tepid beer and wondering what the hell he was doing here in the middle of this primeval debauch of soggy vegetation, this world of snakes and scorpions and primitive, stupid people, where disease and filth and chaos were the accepted, rather than the unacceptable, order of things. His thoughts went back to England and home, as they so often seemed to do these days, and his sense of depression deepened. Right now, on the gentle slopes of his lovely Essex, the corn would be turning to golden bronze and the old men would be out with their scythes, preparing the way for the reapers. He could hear now in his mind the happy summer song of the chaffinch in the high oak tops, the drone of the bumblebee in thick red clover, the measured clack of willow on leather on the village green by the old church spire. How clean and orderly and civilized it all was in the land of his birth, in stark contrast to the squalor of this barbaric land . . .

Murgatroyd was a snob, and Murgatroyd was homesick. He was halfway through his first tour of duty on the Coast, and he didn't know how he was going to make it through the second half. Not even the knowledge that his fiancée, the beautiful Daphne Fairfax, would be sailing out to the Coast to join him in a few months time, could help in any way to lighten his gloom. 'Must be fever coming on', he thought morosely.

He gazed sourly out over the rushing torrent, downstream to where the two colossal okwen trees, one on each side of the river, joined hands a couple of hundred feet above the water. He remembered how, last dry season, the hordes of little grey monkeys from the deep, dark forests to the east had come leaping and dancing and swinging over this natural bridge to lay daily siege to his groves of grapefruit, avocado and banana behind the house. 'The little sods will soon be back again!' he murmured to himself.

The faint but unmistakable sound of African village life intruded on his thoughts: the hoarse, demented call of an elderly rooster, the insistent, effeminate blatting of a goat, the shrill scolding of women, the melancholy wailing of a child. He looked upstream. A misty-blue haze of woodsmoke hung low over the patch of cocoa trees in the middle distance and he could hear the clatter of heavy metal pots and the rhythmic pounding of wooden pestles in mortars. The women of Mundoni were preparing the evening meal. Mundoni Town! 'God bless my soul!' he shuddered aloud. 'Is it really a year since I was last there?' His thoughts flashed back to his one and only visit to the place . . .

He had just arrived on the Coast, fresh from university, brimming with all the grand aspirations of youth and eager to play his part in the preservation of the fabled rainforests of West Africa. He had hated Lagos immediately, with its strident, incessant racket and its gangs of mutilated beggars grabbing at him from every corner, and he had not much liked Ibadan, that great sprawling, black African city of the interior, where his employers, the Forest Department, had their headquarters. There was a large and socially active white community there, and his induction week had seemed to consist of one constant round of parties by night and thick hangovers by day. He was not used to this hectic stuff and long before the week was up he was impatient to leave the city behind him and head for his station in the bush.

He had an unexpected companion on the following Monday morning as the little green forestry truck clattered over the awful rutted track towards the forest boundary. Old Mac, the Chief Conservator of Forests, had decided to come along, on the pretext that he wanted to introduce Murgatroyd to the workforce and his area of responsibility. This, as even a greenhorn like Murgatroyd was well aware, was complete nonsense. There were plenty of people kicking around the headquarter offices who would have been happy to do that minor chore and, in any case, it was hardly the task of a man of such exalted status as Old Mac to be showing the ropes to raw recruits.

But he had heard enough during his short stay in the city to realize that the old man was one of a fast-vanishing breed of bushmen, a man who had himself started off as a forester on the Coast at the end of World War I. Although he had now reached the very pinnacle of his profession, the bush was his first love. Every now and then he would get fed up with his desk job, lock his office door, and go walkabout around the many stations scattered throughout the Nigerian forests. It was a practice not always appreciated by his employees who preferred to have advance warning of impending visits from head office dignitaries. Especially when the dignitary was a cantankerous old martinet such as Old Mac whose taste in expensive whiskies tended to leave large holes in the pockets of his poverty-stricken junior officers after each of his visits.

Mundoni was to be Murgatroyd's responsibility. It was a fairly typical forestry station on the northern fringe of the high forest zone, with an old mud-block bungalow for his own use, a tiny palm-thatched office, and a lean-to garage to provide shade for his transport. It was apparent from the beginning that his work would tax him neither physically or mentally. For the most part, it would involve the supervision of a few small gangs of workers armed with machetes, who were engaged in the clearing of lianas and assorted weed-species from experimental plots in the forest, in order to give more easily suppressed species such as the mahoganies a better chance of survival. The upkeep of basic records and a monthly trip to the city for supplies and workers' wages would provide just about the only diversion from this routine.

Before he departed to harass some other hapless victim, Old Mac took Murgatroyd on a tour of Mundoni Town. Originally intended as a base for the housing of forestry staff, Mundoni had rapidly degenerated from being a neat, orderly little camp of some 30 cement-faced, mud-block huts with roofs of thatch, into a horrible little shantytown of some 150 shacks in various stages of disrepair. Hunters, fishermen, farmers and traders from all points of the compass had converged on the place, building huts for their wives, clearing patches of forest to make way for their yam and cocoa farms. Cocoa had brought prosperity to a few of them too: a few of the larger dwellings were roofed with corrugated iron, and corrugated iron was a sign of affluence on the Coast in those days.

The frightful squalor of the place repelled him. Open sewers, seething with blowflies, bubbled and stewed in the heat. Tiny, naked children, bellies grotesquely swollen, crawled in the sludge, and skeletal curs slunk around the doorways, gobbling up whatever excrement attracted their attention. The smell was quite overpowering – an evil macedoine of drying stockfish and cocoa beans, rotting fruit and vegetables, decaying rats and – inextricably intermingled with all the other odours – the penetrating stench of vaporizing urine and human excreta.

Murgatroyd could hardly wait to get out of the place, but Old Mac was enjoying himself immensely. He spoke to everyone they met, greeting them all with easy familiarity, rubbing the crinkly heads of the children and teasing the old mammies unmercifully. He had been here before and he was obviously hugely popular. Not for the first time in his life, Murgatroyd felt a faint twinge of regret at his own traditional reserve. They ended their tour of the town at the grandly named Julie Mundoni Hotel. This was a low-roofed, rambling edifice of mud and wattle and scraps of rusting tin that sold bottles of beer, illicit gin, candles, paraffin, matches, tins of sardines, bundles of tobacco leaves, and an assortment of other bric-a-brac. Old Julie Mundoni herself, a veritable mountain of rotund black flesh, met them at the door, beaming widely. Somewhere over in the corner of the capacious bar a gramophone started up with a scratchy rendering of African high-life music and, as though they had emerged from cracks in the mud wall, half a dozen young girls, bare from the waist up but clad in colourful print skirts, appeared and stared curiously at them, giggling at Murgatroyd's obvious discomfort until Julie Mundoni scattered them with a verbal salvo.

They sat down at a rough plank table. Julie Mundoni brought Murgatroyd a bottle of warm beer and a filthy glass and set them down before him. The old man, eschewing such sophistication, opted for a jug of palm wine. Murgatroyd had never felt so uncomfortable in his life. The old man, on the other hand, was quite obviously in his element. He lifted his palm wine to his mouth, gulping down the thick, floury goo with the relish that he might have accorded a particularly fine malt from his favourite distillery back home in those far-off glens.

The girls had begun to dance, shuffling round the floor in front of them, their hip movements graceful, fluid and erotically teasing. One of them called out to them, signalling them to join them on the floor. Old Mac stood up, wiped the palm wine from his white moustache, and escorted Julie Mundoni onto the floor on his arm with old-world gallantry. Murgatroyd watched in amazement as his boss, a ferocious disciplinarian at work and the debonair doyen of the social set by night back in the city, now waltzed old Julie around the dirt floor of this ramshackle dive in the middle of nowhere, whispering God knows what scandalous things in her ear so that her body shook all over with laughter, like some black unidentifiable, gelatinous mass floating on a stormy sea. Within minutes the old man had reduced the dancing to a shambles as he cavorted among the girls, slapping bottoms and tweaking nipples *en passant* until all of them had fled, shrieking with laughter, back through the curtains behind the bar.

Murgatroyd was scarlet with embarrassment at his chief's antics.

The music ended and Old Mac escorted Julie Mundoni back to the table. Murgatroyd reached for his drink. Two fat bluebottles, copulating on the rim of his tumbler, fell into the beer. He pushed the glass away from him, revolted. Julie Mundoni reached across and dipped a large, fat forefinger into the froth in his glass. 'Excuse me!' she said. She fished out the flies and squashed them on the table with her thumb. The crack of the bursting bodies was audible. 'We can't have flies shitting in your beer,' she explained succinctly. Even now, one year later, his stomach lurched queasily at the memory . . .

He was roused from his reverie by a cough at his elbow. He turned irritably to find Musa, his houseboy, proffering a letter. He looked at the neat, handwritten address on the envelope: 'To The Manager of Mundoni'

Puzzled, he opened it and took out a sheet of typewritten paper. He unfolded it and began reading.

To: The Manager of Mundoni,
From: The Harlots of Mundoni . . .

He read no further.

'MUSA!!!' His stentorian bellow of outrage sent clouds of yellow weaver birds whirring out of the mango tree down by the river and brought Musa back to his side in a trice. 'What the hell is this rubbish?' he blared. 'And who brought this letter?'

'One man called David Ojo, Sir.'

David Ojo, his much-respected senior foreman. How very odd! He read on with growing incredulity.

Dear Manager,
Although we are Harlots, we are not as black as we are painted. But one Gemima Elijah has come into our midst and she has blackened our names with an ink that cannot be milted out. Being from the city, she is more beautiful than we bush girls. And she wears fine-fine European cloth. Also, she charges less money for her harlotry.

But, Mr Manager, the biggest shame of all is that she refuses to join our Harlot's Union. In fact, she uses very bad language when we ask her for Union Dues. The men laugh at us now and all have gone on transfer to Gemima Elijah. She has taken our business night and day and has brought shame to our house. Also, she says that even the Manager has no power over her.

We beg the Manager to use all his power to put Gemima Elijah underneath him forever.

May the Lord guide your footsteps in our direction.

We are,
Yours faithfully,
The Harlots of Mundoni.

PS. If the Manager wishes to know more about our character, he should ask the bearer of this letter, Mr David Ojo

Ten names were typed at the bottom of the letter and, opposite each, an inky thumb print, the traditional 'Coast signature'. John Murgatroyd leaned back in his chair, eyes closed, his mind awhirl. Then he issued the only two sensible commands he could think of.

'Musa . . . bring me the whisky and soda. Then go and fetch David Ojo.'

David Ojo stood before him. He eyed the tall foreman pensively. Slender, handsome and highly intelligent, the Ibo personified all that was best in his race. He was, Murgatroyd felt, far too smart to be a mere foreman over a motley collection of labourers in a forestry plantation in the middle of nowhere. But he disliked the city life and city people, and an attempt by Old Mac to teach him something of the mechanics of administration back in headquarters had ended in a near riot when the Ibo's infamous temper had got the better of him and he had attempted to eviscerate three supercilious office clerks with his machete. He had escaped instant dismissal and a jail sentence only through Old Mac's intervention, the old man stating that the Ibo had only been trying to do what he himself had been wanting to do for years. So David Ojo had landed back in the bush, and he had expressed no desire ever to leave it again. Murgatroyd liked and trusted him, and over the past year he had come to rely greatly on his local knowledge and advice.

'You have read the letter?' Murgatroyd prompted.

'Yes, Sir' Ojo replied.

'Have you had any . . . er . . . dealings with these women?' he queried.

'Sir, I only know of them. I do not sleep with harlots,' said David Ojo loftily.

There was a long pause as they looked at each other. 'Right then, David,' resumed Murgatroyd briskly to conceal the wave of embarrassment that was sweeping over him, 'let's get down to brass tacks. What's the real problem?'

'Well, Sir,' began his foreman, 'in Africa, we have a pidgin-English saying which goes 'Man-fowl, he no de maka wahalla in other man-fowl he compound'. That is to say, only a very foolish cockerel would dare to trespass on another's territory and think he could rule the roost there. Strangers in strange lands should maintain a low profile and they should be prepared to obey the laws existing in that land. Gemima Elijah has done neither. She has come into Mundoni Town as a stranger from the city and already she acts as though she were queen of Mundoni.'

'But surely,' objected Murgatroyd, 'that is a matter for the town of Mundoni to resolve? It has nothing to do with me!'

'You have only been in our country for a year,' retorted David Ojo, and there was an rising edge of temper in his voice. 'You know nothing of our ways. When women make war with each other anywhere, there is always trouble. In a bush town like Mundoni, it is worse, for it affects everyone. The Harlots are a very essential part of our lives here. They keep our young men happy, but at the same time, they have a code of honour and they don't mess around with our married ones. And by forming their Harlot's Union they have ensured that there is a sharing of their workload and an equal division of their earnings. With Gemima Elijah, it is a free-for-all, and she has disrupted the whole social fabric of our community. Even our work is suffering as a result – our workers are starting to take time off to be with her by day. There is a lot of jealousy too; they are beginning to quarrel over her and I am afraid that before long there will be bloodshed. Gemima Elijah must be made to toe the line or leave!'

Murgatroyd stared at him silently, digesting this extraordinary tirade. He reflected wryly that his august *alma mater*, excellently though it had served him in all departments appertaining to his chosen career, had ill-prepared him on the subject of Harlot's Unions. But perhaps his foreman had a point; work had certainly been slipshod of late and absenteeism high.

'All right, David Ojo,' he said finally, 'you obviously have some ideas on the subject. What do you suggest we should do about it?'

'The town had its beginnings as a forestry camp,' said David Ojo, 'and it remains basically so today. Because of that, it has many different races and, for the same reason, it has no proper chief, otherwise this dispute would have been settled long ago. You are our boss, so we also look on you as being the boss of all Mundoni. I believe that Gemima Elijah will listen to you, so if you will undertake to speak privately to her, telling her that she must obey the town laws or leave the area, I will tell the Mundoni elders that they have your support. Also, I will ask the Harlots to refrain from making trouble until we see how Gemima Elijah will react.'

'One thing I am curious about,' said Murgatroyd pensively, 'what exactly is your interest in the matter?'

'No interest at all, Sir,' replied his foreman virtuously, 'except that our work should not be disrupted. Also . . .'

'Yes?'

'Well, Sir, Julie Mundoni and I get married next week, and the Harlots have their headquarters in her hotel . . .'

He slept fitfully, and woke in the grey light of dawn with a splitting headache. He lay still for a few minutes, undecided whether it was the onset of malaria, or the effects of too much whisky the night before, or that infernal Gemima Elijah problem that was the cause of it. Probably all three, he thought gloomily. He swallowed a couple of tablets and got out of bed. Over his morning cup of tea he pondered on the events of yesterday and the more he pondered the less he liked the idea of having any truck with that horrible little town and its problems. He mulled over a number of ways in which he might be able to extract himself from all the unpleasantness and still be able to retain the respect of David Ojo and his workers. Finally, he decided that there was nothing for it but to get the whole sordid business over and done with. He called for Musa.

'Do you know one Gemima Elijah from Mundoni Town?'

'I have heard her name,' replied his houseboy cautiously.

'Then bring her back here for me now!'

'Sir?'

'You heard me! Go to Mundoni Town and tell Gemima Elijah that the manager wants her here. Immediately!'

Musa departed. Murgatroyd poured himself more tea and settled back to await the arrival of the infamous Gemima Elijah.

She was, in fact, a remarkably attractive little thing by any standard. The garish slash of lipstick across her dusky features did little to detract from the beauty of a face quite unblemished by her hectic lifestyle. A short, bright-yellow skirt and a tight-fitting scarlet top gave disturbing emphasis to a figure that looked little short of perfection. Her smile was absolutely dazzling. With a sudden jolt of panic, he realized that she had completely misconstrued the reason for her summons to his house. She had assumed this to be a call to arms, a promotion from the stresses and stratagems of the town to the haven of the managerial boudoir and a glowing future as Mistress of Mundoni. One in the eye for the Harlots, indeed!

He shrugged off his growing sense of despair at what he had got himself involved in and launched into his prepared speech, speaking with a cold, detached venom that he certainly did not feel. Her departure a few minutes later in a flood of tears left him feeling quite wretched for the rest of the day.

In the weeks that followed, however, tranquillity returned to the forests of Mundoni. Murgatroyd noticed it at work. The men were back to their old jocular, mischievous ways and there was a palpable lack of tension in the air. He and David Ojo met quite often in the course of duty, but their conversation was mainly about work. On a number of occasions he was about to say something to the foreman about the Mundoni problem, but the words just would not come out. Finally, he could no longer contain his curiosity. He broached the subject almost diffidently:

'David, about that Mundoni business you asked me to help you with – I take it that the whole palaver is now settled?'

'Oh yes, Sir,' replied the foreman. 'Completely settled. The Harlots are very grateful to you.'

Something was still troubling Murgatroyd. His mind kept returning to that miserable morning when a pretty young girl with high aspirations had dressed in her finest clothes especially for him. Hesitantly, he put his final question to the foreman, for some unaccountable reason almost dreading what the reply might be: 'What happened to Gemima Elijah in the end?'

David Ojo chipped aimlessly at a sapling with his machete, not looking directly at Murgatroyd, forming his sentences with care. 'Well, Sir, you will remember that I married Julie Mundoni earlier in the year? She is, of course, rather old; it was what you English would call a marriage of convenience. She is rich, and I needed money badly at the time. She is very good to me, but I am a young man, and young men need young women to satisfy their worldly desires. So . . .'

In dawning comprehension, Murgatroyd gasped: 'You don't mean . . . ?'

'Yes, Sir,' replied David Ojo. 'Gemima Elijah became my second wife two weeks ago.'

I suppose this story, had it been fiction, would have ended there and then for Murgatroyd, with the Mundoni business all settled, David Ojo's domestic affairs running smoothly, and his own lady coming out in a few weeks' time for Christmas. But this is not fiction, and stories with perfect endings are few and far between in Africa, as those of us who have given the best part of lives to the Coast know only too well. Mother Africa is, at times, a malicious old meddler, and there are occasions when she just cannot leave well alone. This was one of those, and the reason I am in a position to tell this story is that, many years after it had all happened, it was related to me in the Enugu Expatriate Club by one of Old Mac's forestry officers who had been on a temporary posting to Mundoni at the time of the dénouement:

On Christmas Day John Murgatroyd sat on his verandah, gazing with pride and adoration at his brand-new wife. They had been married the previous week in Lagos, and it had been an event of quite grandiose splendour. The bride's mother had sailed out from England for the wedding and, as Daphne's father had died many years ago, Old Mac had been accorded the honour of giving the bride away. As might have been expected, he had carried out his duties with an elegance and charm that belonged to a different age. Indeed, the attention that the courtly old gallant had paid to the bride's mother at the reception afterwards had had that formidable dowager fluttering round like a starry-eyed adolescent for days afterwards.

A few days after the ceremony Murgatroyd and his wife had set off up country, at her request, to spend part of their honeymoon at Murgatroyd's station in the Mundoni forests. She looked absolutely stunning now, thought Murgatroyd, as they sat together in the cool of the morning. A crowd of inquisitive Mundoni children thronged around the verandah rail, staring wide-eyed at the first white woman they had ever seen in their lives.

All around them were scattered the traditional seasonal gifts sent by minor chiefs, elders, farmers, hunters and fishermen from far and near. The house and surroundings were littered with gifts of all kinds – squat, surly-looking black ducks, scrawny white chickens trussed up resignedly in the corner of the verandah, baskets of eggs, pineapples, oranges, mangoes and yams. Tethered to a guava bush out in the compound, bleating pathetically, was one small goat. As each bearer came in, she thanked him graciously and gave him a token gift of her own. At the end of the line was a small naked child who came shyly to her and, to Murgatroyd's astonishment, laid a bottle of Scotch whisky at her feet.

'Good Lord!' he exclaimed, 'who sent that?' The child,

uncomprehending, stood there nervously on one foot like a stork, eyes darting hither and thither, clearly wishing he was anywhere but here in such close proximity to two white people. Daphne reached out her hand to the boy to draw him closer to her. Like a flash, he was off the verandah and gone, bouncing across the compound like a springbok, to vanish into the sanctuary of the trees.

'There's a label attached to the neck of the bottle, darling,' Murgatroyd pointed out. 'What does it say?'

She picked the bottle up and, as she read, her smile froze. The bottle fell from her nerveless grasp and she stared at him, her face a mixture of incredulity, horror and shock. 'What the . . . ?' Murgatroyd ejaculated as he rose from his chair. But, before he could reach her, she had spun round, tears welling in her eyes, and fled to her room. The door was slammed in his face and the key turned in the lock.

Thoroughly mystified, he returned to the verandah and picked up the bottle. The writing on the label was vaguely familiar, and, as he read, it danced before his eyes like the jig of a newly-hanged man. The message was simple and seasonal:

Greetings and Merry Christmas.

To — The Manager of Mundoni,
From — The Harlots of Mundoni.
For Services Rendered.

Chapter 18
JAM PASS DIE

'Jam pass die, monkey chop peppeh.'
(Pidgin English: A starving monkey will even eat peppers)

A steady stream of migrant butterflies flew over the compound, a never-ending, rolling wave of them, all heading inexorably in the same direction, stopping for nothing. Pale-green, fragile creatures, fluttering along in jerky, dipping, jigging flight over the short wiry grass. At the far end of the compound the light-green wave rose in a gentle arc, clearing the guava bushes in front of the old boys' quarters, then faded slowly from sight in the shadows of the two mighty silver-barked silk-cotton trees growing side by side on the bank of the hidden stream.

They flew laboriously, as butterflies do, but this was not the aimless, zigzag flight of the ordinary butterfly. This flight had an air of purpose to it, as though the participants sensed they were heading towards the fulfilment of some great destiny up there in the north beyond the swamps, forests, savannahs and sand dunes. Only God Himself knew where they were going and why they were embarked on this incredible journey. I doubt if the butterflies themselves knew; I certainly didn't, and I never met anyone else who ever did either. All I knew for sure was that this mass exodus would continue for the best part of the afternoon. I knew that it would, because I had seen it all before.

I had, in fact, seen it once before, and once only. Twenty-five years before, to be precise, and from this very vantage point. It had been Christmas Day then too and, just as now, I had been sitting on this verandah on my own. Twenty-five years ago they had flown over this same compound, heading north, like a great elfin nation on the move. I had timed them, and it had been almost three hours before this tidal wave of butterflies had dwindled to a trickle, and a further hour before the trickle had become nothing more than a few pale stragglers struggling along pathetically in the wake of the multitude.

I returned to my chair. A pair of swallows flashed past the back of my head and along the length of the verandah, twittering excitedly. A split second later they were back and gone in a shimmering blur of royal-blue and russet-orange into the heavens. They were European swallows, fleeing the winter blasts of the frozen north for a few brief months of sunshine with their African cousins. Their forebears had been here too, on that hot December day of long ago, and they had greeted me in exactly the same way.

All nature seemed to be on the move and I was restless myself. I had no idea why; it was just a vague, indefinable inner restiveness that had been with me lately, a restiveness that had impelled me to embark on this long journey back through the lands where my African odyssey had carried me all these years ago. And now I was back to my very beginnings, back to the house where I had spent my first night in the bush, and I was still restive. What were the gods trying to tell me? I mused. Were they trying to tell me that it was time that I, too, packed my bags and went? That a quarter of a century on the White Man's Grave was long enough for any man and it was time I returned to the land of my birth? Or were they trying to show me that, despite my misgivings, nothing much had changed here since the days of my youth? That a few trees may have gone, but Africa and her multifarious inhabitants were the same as they had always been, doing the things they had always done since time began, and that this would never change? Was that it?

I looked around me. Quite a lot had changed in my immediate surroundings, that was for sure. The house was still there, but only just. It was little more than a tumbledown shack now, and it was filthy. Great strings of cobwebs hung like fishing nets from the rafters, and there was a six-inch deep pile of bat droppings on the floor under the arch between kitchen and living room. The few bits of furniture remaining were layered thick with dust and some of the floorboards had rotted away. An odour of mould and decay pervaded the whole place but this, I supposed, was only to be expected. The house had had no permanent occupant these past four or five years. It was now being used as a rest-house by touring government officers and, judging by the state of the place, they didn't come around this way too often.

Much the same could have been said of the surrounding landscape. As with the house, there was an appearance of crumbling decay about everything, as though some cataclysmic hurricane had swept through in the distant past and no one had bothered to clean up after it. The compound grass had been cropped short by the small herd of village goats that had obviously made their headquarters there, but that was the only good thing they had done. They had equally happily dined on the hibiscus and all the other flowering shrubs that had provided such a blaze of colour around the house when it had been occupied long ago by generations of timber people. Even the sprawling bougainvillea, which I could remember as having been a riot of glorious purple when it had formed a thick arch over the verandah steps in the old days, had been reduced to a mass of desiccated thorns, its bark and its life long since chewed away by the voracious creatures.

But the biggest change of all was to be seen beyond the bounds of the compound. Twenty-five years ago the house had been completely surrounded by the dark-crowned trees of West Africa, all the typical tree species to be found in the rainforest flatlands. Lagoswood, brimstone, agba, ironwood, sasswood, okwen, dibetou, ako, apa – these, and many more like them, had crowded in on the bungalow on all sides. Some of the early Europeans had not liked it much here, saying that the proximity of this dark and forbidding wall of forest gave the house and the compound a crypt-like feel. It was a permanent air of gloom that encouraged thick, cloying mists that seldom evaporated and through which the sun rarely penetrated. They would not have had much to complain about now, I reckoned. Apart from the two cotton trees at the foot of the compound, the horizon on all sides was bare of trees of any kind. They had vanished long ago in the name of progress, to be replaced by patches of cassava and plantain and a jungle of sawgrass and wait-a-bit thorns. The trees had gone, and with them a way of life for everything that had been ordained to work and play and hunt in their deep, wet shadows.

A cynic once remarked to me that one should never overlook the significance of the fact that the greatest man-made disasters ever to descend upon the shores of the White Man's Grave were the three that arrived during the same decade and with equally dire consequences for the old way of life: independence, the telex and the chainsaw. It was not a view to which I subscribed in its entirety, but then he was a die-hard Old Coaster, very much steeped in the traditions of Lord Lugard and Rudyard Kipling, not to mention the pint or so of pink gin in which he was also steeped when he was expounding his theories to me. Independence for the African nations was as inevitable as it was necessary. Everyone likes to peel his own banana, to quote an old African saying, and those Empire wallahs who sneered at the violent birth pangs of the emergent nations were conveniently forgetting the bloodletting that had continued long after the birth of their own nation.

But the telex and the chainsaw were linked, for they were part of a new technology that heralded the modern era of speed and efficiency for the Coast. In those days it often took weeks on end to get 'urgent' messages from Europe to the man in the bush. An irate timber executive in London wondering what the hell was happening about that parcel of logs he had ordered last year would fire off an agitated letter to his manager out on the Coast, and he would become even more irate – but not very surprised – to receive in return some three weeks later a missive with the brief query 'What?' on it. Such insouciance on the part of the old-time bushman of West Africa – his two-fingered joy at his isolation and consequent unaccountability – became almost part of folklore. He was a white king in a black man's world.

The telex changed all that, and it went hand-in-hand with the chainsaw in doing so. The timber barons of Europe wanted answers NOW, and they expected their logs NOW – not whenever the Coast bushman felt like it. Far from being the free spirit he once was, he now became a mere cipher, the flunkey who kept the machine oiled. The telex and the chainsaw together ensured that the barons got what they wanted, faster and faster and in greater and greater quantity. But, with all this high-tech speed and efficiency came high-tech corruption.

The rich diversity of timber species within the forests of the Coast provided a marvellous opportunity for graft on a grand scale. Corruption in a number of these emergent nations was rife, and it was to be found in all ranks, from the most minor official to the highest level of government. Lowly forest guards would be paid 'expenses' by the very timber company whose activities their own government employers had paid them to supervise. Often these 'expenses' would amount to three or four times the value of their actual salary. In return, the guard would be expected to turn a blind eye to any indiscretion committed by the logging company concerned. Needless to say, the forest guard's immediate superior would expect a correspondingly higher remuneration for keeping his mouth shut. What it meant, in effect, was that these junior officials were being paid substantial sums of money just to stay in their homes all day long and play with their girlfriends while the logging company concerned proceeded unhindered with its activities. When official documents appertaining to the company's operations had to be signed and stamped by a forest guard, they would simply be brought to his door later that evening by the company's representative. Forest guards were among the fattest, laziest and richest people I knew on the Coast in the years after independence.

Unfortunately, this sort of extortion did not always stop with those junior officials. In at least a few of the new nations, it was to be found at ministerial level. It is significant that the two posts most sought after in government by ambitious politicians were those of Minister of Forestry and Minister of Finance. This was not always, alas, because certain politicians had suddenly been smitten by pangs of conscience over the decimation of their nation's natural resources, or by a dream that theirs was the destiny to halt their country's current plunge into the abyss of insolvency. Often, it had much more to do with the state of their own personal finances. They were on the lookout for kickbacks, and there were timber companies around who were only too willing to take advantage of their greed.

In some countries this overt corruption went to even higher levels than that of cabinet minister. I was present myself on one occasion when the world-renowned head of one nation was offered a very substantial monetary 'gift' by the owner of an acquisitive logging company seeking permission to obtain the right to fell a large tract of virgin mahogany forest deep in the heart of elephant country. The gift was accepted with alacrity and with no visible trace of embarrassment by the august ruler. The following week the timber company moved in with their chainsaws.

The fact that this particular despot was assassinated a few months later by someone even more corrupt than he, but who nevertheless succeeded in ruling the roost in his place for years afterwards before he, too, was shot, is a pretty fair indication of how difficult it must have been for anyone with even the most casual of moral standards to derive any job satisfaction from operating within those regimes.

There were timber companies that did manage to avoid floundering around in this sea of sleaze. One of the few whose record remained untarnished was the United Africa Company. But then, they were big boys. They had sole felling rights to vast tracts of forest on the Coast long before the day of independence arrived for any of the West African countries. Besides, as part of the giant Unilever structure, they had an international reputation to maintain. Even had they felt inclined – which they certainly didn't – they couldn't afford to risk their good name by dipping their toes in those murky waters. So they kept their imperial noses high in the air, paid their dues officially, correctly and on time, and extracted from the forests the timbers to which they were entitled by law and no more than that.

One or two of the smaller companies also managed to keep their heads above it all, but many succumbed to the rampant corruption. To be fair, many of those who were not so squeaky-clean were small concerns that were simply trying to stay alive, firms that simply couldn't afford not to be involved in the shenanigans going on all around them. The others were all doing it, they argued, and if they didn't, there would be no slice of the cake for them. All to often, this was indeed what happened.

Corruption did not begin with the introduction of the telex and the chainsaw to the Coast. It was there before that. But everything — including the corruption — moved an awful lot faster from that point onward. A tree that had taken a couple of days to fell with axes could now be flattened within minutes. Machines for moving logs from stump to loading point became bigger and faster and more sophisticated. Timber lorries, from being stumpy little trucks loaded with three or four tons of logs, became massive juggernauts capable of carrying upwards of 40 tons at a time while travelling at fearsome speed. A sudden encounter with one of those leviathans piled high with giant logs and moving at something just short of the speed of sound on a narrow logging track, was an experience not readily forgotten.

The demand for timber of all kinds escalated rapidly. Now it was not only the mahoganies and their substitutes that were being sought. Ply mills were looking for just about anything that was big, straight and cylindrical of body, was reasonably soft of texture, and could hold glue well. Colour became irrelevant. Suddenly, species that had been ignored by generations of timber men became all-important. Obeche, with its white, satin-smooth wood, and the lustrous, yellowish-green framiré, were now just as much in demand as the mahoganies. Where previously only around half-a-dozen species were of any interest to the timber trade, now the forests were being combed for new possibilities. The race was on and the timber pirates multiplied, scrapping like piranhas for every stick of saleable wood they could find.

And in every country bordering the Gulf of Guinea, from the Mano to the Cuanzo rivers, the chainsaws shrieked and whined and howled their eldritch dirges and spewed their noisome vapours while the forests trembled at their approach . . .

The butterflies had gone now and there was nothing left in the compound to indicate that they had ever been there. The sun was sinking in a huge red ball of fire behind the cassava tops and flights of swallows were darting and flickering in the evening air, gorging themselves on invisible insects.

A faint, familiar sound came to my ears. I strained my eyes to the south, above and beyond the thickets of plantains and into the fading blue of the horizon skies. Finally, he hove into view, whistling, calling and chattering – a parrot on the lookout for a berth for the night. He dipped suddenly over the cotton trees, wheeling in a wide arc above them, each circuit lower than the last, flying with the rapid, pigeon-like wing beats that parrots have. A long, dead branch at the top of the taller of the two trees attracted his attention and he alighted on it suddenly and with easy grace. He stretched his wings once, then crab-walked along the branch to the tip, still engaged in non-stop conversation with – so far as I could ascertain from my own perch – no one in particular but himself.

I rose and went through into the kitchen. A rickety old paraffin refrigerator stood in the corner. I opened it and a blast of cold air gushed out. Amazing, I reflected, how these battered old relics always operated more efficiently than the newer ones. It was empty apart from three bottles of water, obviously put there by the caretaker some time ago against the event of the arrival of surprise guests such as myself. The bottles were freezing cold. I took one out, then rummaged around in my rucksack until I found what I was looking for. I pulled out the bottle of whisky and went back to the verandah to await the arrival of the caretaker.

The whisky was mellow and soothing. My earlier depression was lifting. I allowed my mind to wander back again over the years, this time lingering a good deal longer on the good times, as is the privilege of men who have reached a certain maturity of years despite all the odds. I thought about the characters I had met during my time on the Coast, characters with names like Serious Business, Iron Bar and Money-Done-Finish. Where on earth had they got those names from? I wondered. And where were they now? What had happened to Magic

Sperm and Old Man Africa? Had they gone too, along with the trees and the animals and the birds?

I remembered Famous Sixpence. When I first met him somewhere along the Grain Coast he was senile, so old that he tottered rather than walked. I was in urgent need of a general dogsbody at the time, someone who could make the odd cup of tea for me and take care of my house during my prolonged absences. Famous Sixpence had been recommended so, as there did not seem to be anyone else available, I hired him.

He was a nice old boy, but he was illiterate and disaster-prone. He had had a varied career, serving as a houseboy and caretaker for a heterogeneous collection of missionaries and rubber planters. His only real attribute was his honesty. He was a terrible cook and his eyesight was so bad as to make him an environmental hazard. On one memorable occasion, just after the introduction of gas canisters into the kitchens of expatriate homes in the area, he all but blew the two of us into outer space. A colossal explosion brought me flying in from the compound to find Famous Sixpence miraculously still in one piece, sitting dazed on the floor amidst the wreckage of my kitchen. 'When I hear WHISSHH sound like snake coming from the corner,' he explained afterwards, 'I light candle to try to find it.'

Famous Sixpence was not with me for long, and I never found out why he was called 'Sixpence'. But it was quite a common name in this part of Africa, so I suppose I never gave too much thought to the matter. Nor did I spend a lot of time pondering on the 'Famous' part of it, and, remarkably, it was not until the end of our association that I was made aware of its derivation. His first employer, he informed me, had been Mary Kingsley, the renowned traveller. My face must have registered some disbelief, because he then invited me to come down to his house on this, our last day together, to drink palm wine with him and see his 'reference.'

That night, in his little house by the sea, he told me the story. His father had been a cook in Cameroon for the then German Governor, and Sixpence – then only a little boy – had been given the task of looking after the explorer during her stay in Victoria. His duties were not too onerous: his sole task was to keep her chalet clean.

'How long did you work for her?' I asked, intrigued.

'One day,' he replied.

'One *day*?'

'Yes sir. One day.'

It was a poignant tale. Her chalet, having been unoccupied for some time, was badly in need of a good clean out. She dumped all her gear in it and left him to it. Sixpence swept it out from top to bottom. Hornet nests, bat droppings, old papers, dead mice and even deader lizards – everything ended up on the bonfire Sixpence had lit outside in the compound. The whole house sparkled like a new pin when Miss Kingsley returned that evening.

Here Sixpence paused, and I sensed that this story was reaching a dramatic conclusion. 'So?' I prompted.

'Then she fired me,' he said.

'*Fired* you! But why?' I asked.

'Well,' replied the old man sadly, 'inside her cupboard I see one big box with plenty dead "bugga-bugga" in it. So . . .'

'Good God!' I exclaimed. 'Not her insect collection for the British Museum! You didn't chuck them on the fire?'

'I was only a small boy then,' said Famous Sixpence defensively.

I could think of nothing adequate to say for a moment or two. Then I asked curiously: 'What did she say to you?'

'She called me a bloody fool,' he said frankly.

The room fell silent. Then the old man opened a folder on the table beside him. 'I been keeping this to show you,' he said, extracting with great care a fragile, yellowed scrap of paper. 'This is my reference from Miss Kingsley,' he told me proudly. I opened the faded document and read:

> This is to certify that during his eight hours in my employ, Mr Sixpence has
> succeeded in exercising my mind in a way that no one else has ever done.
> To those seeking stimulus from the daily ennui of life on the Coast,
> I recommend him.

The signature was indecipherable.

Famous Sixpence shuffled over to the window and looked out at the stars. 'She was a very wonderful woman,' he murmured distantly.

The coming of darkness had silenced the parrot. The only sounds to be heard now were the fricative churrings of the cicadas out there in the warm night air and the spitting of the storm lantern I had lit at the end of the verandah. That damned caretaker had still not arrived and I wondered where he had got to. When I had called at his house in the village earlier that day his wife had given me the key to the door of the rest-house, saying that her husband had gone to his farm but would be along to see me 'soon' to prepare the place for me. The Coast still operated on 'Africa Time', I reflected irritably.

I reached for the whisky, still brooding on the past. I remembered the forests of my youth, remembered them as they had been before they had begun to melt away like snow in Scottish mountain corries with the summer sun upon them. I remembered the elephant and the leopard and the chimpanzee and the aardvark, remembered the time when they had roamed free through the forest mists, remembered how the high tops and the skies above them had echoed hourly to the calls of hoopoe, touraco and bateleur. Now, they had vanished with the forests, ousted by the greed and the mechanics of man.

But it had not all been bad news, at least, not for the people of the interior. Roads built by timber companies to extract timber were now being used by mammy-waggons to take the people of the more remote areas to and from market. Medical clinics could now be found in the most unlikely of places, vaccinating and inoculating against diseases that, in my time, had wiped out whole communities. The old-fashioned witch doctor, if he had not entirely disappeared, had had his influence greatly reduced. Now, he was just as likely to be a patient at the government clinic himself when his own potions failed to deliver.

Schools, too, were springing up everywhere, bringing hope to a new generation of African. Education had spread like wildfire, and the winds of change were fanning those flames. The greatest change was in the role of woman. No longer was she prepared to be hacked about in some archaic circumcision rite by a savage old witch wielding a rusty knife or a sliver of glass. She, too, was going to school and learning about the world outside Africa, and she was fast figuring out that there was a little more to life than being tenth wife to some toothless old village chief living in a mud hut in the back of beyond. This was a brand-new Africa, and we from its past – the witch doctors, the village chiefs, myself – were as redundant as the dinosaur in the making of it.

I was reaching for the bottle of Scotch again when I heard the shuffle of footsteps on the ground outside. An old black man climbed stiffly up the verandah steps and stood before me, a calabash in his hand. White froth around the spout told me that it was full to the brim with palm wine. He placed it on the floor beside me, grinning broadly. 'Welcome, Massa!' he greeted me. 'My wife told me that there was a white stranger at the rest-house. Sorry about my lateness.' He stood uncertainly before me, then he continued: 'My daughter will soon be coming with some food for you.'

I thanked him and motioned for him to sit down on the chair beside me. My annoyance at his lateness had completely evaporated. I went through to the kitchen and returned with three glasses. I filled two of them with palm wine, keeping one to myself and handing the other to him. Then I poured a large measure of whisky into the third glass and handed that also to him. He drained it at a gulp and I refilled his glass. He was peering at me perplexedly in the flickering light. Then his jaw dropped open in incredulity.

'I remember you now! Twenty years ago! We were together! On the river!' He was beside himself with excitement. 'Wel-i-come, Massa! Wel-i-come!' Then, seeing the blank look on my face, he continued: 'Don't you remember me? I was your canoe man . . . Pisspot!'

Pisspot! Of course! I certainly had the most vivid memories of him. I had been working about 100 miles north of where we now sat, and I had engaged him as a canoe man. It was only after I had hired him that I discovered that his penchant for tippling far exceeded his capacity for work. He was never sober and he was a dangerous liability as a canoe man. I should have dispensed with his services in the beginning, but he was such a likeable character that I hadn't the heart.

Inevitably, his drinking was to be our undoing in the end. We were travelling down a badly swollen river to a new campsite. His canoe was heavily laden with my gear and Pisspot, as a precaution against sudden, prolonged droughts, had brought along a couple of dozen bottles of his favourite and most toxic hooch. Reaching over the mountain of equipment in the canoe for one of the bottles, he had inadvertently dropped his paddle in the water, where, being made of ironwood, it had sunk like a stone. In the ensuing scramble, I, too, had gone overboard. My last view of Pisspot – as, by the grace of God, I had found myself being swept rapidly to the bank – had been of him sitting on a tarpaulin with a bottle in his hand as the canoe spun out of control round a bend in the river. A subsequent and rather cursory search of each bank by the police had found trace of neither him nor the canoe and it was assumed that he had perished in the rapids further downstream, a fate all too common among even abstemious watermen on that stretch of river in those days. Now here he was, standing in front of me, pumping my hand up and down and beaming at me as though I were a long lost brother.

He sat down beside me again, grinning into my face like an imbecile. 'Pisspot,' I said severely, 'I don't know why I am even talking to you. I nearly died because of your drunkenness. I can't swim, you know!'

Pisspot picked up his tumbler. It was empty again. He stared at the whisky bottle. Reluctantly, I passed it over. He filled his glass to the brim. 'Massa,' he said, 'on that morning there were two of us who couldn't swim for different reasons, but we still made it to the shore!'

I gazed out over the verandah rail and into the night sky. A huge African moon was edging its way up behind the two cotton trees, bathing the compound in silvery light and velvet shadow. Beyond the trees and down in the village a lone drummer began to beat a vigorous tattoo. A second drummer picked up the beat, hesitantly at first, then faster and more confidently, until the two merged as one in the ancient rhythm. They were warming up for the dance that was being held this night in the village compound, one to which I had received a warm invitation on my arrival.

A slender young woman, balancing a large, covered pan of food on her head, appeared at the foot of the verandah steps. Even from where I sat I could smell the rich aroma of palm oil and fragrant spices. She greeted me shyly, laid the pan down gently at my feet, then, without another word, she moved off into the darkness of the house. I began to hear the welcome sounds of feminine organization behind me: the hiss of the big gas lamp being lit, the harsh scraping of her rattan broom, the creaking of floorboards as she fixed the mosquito net around the big iron rest-house bed.

Pisspot was filling his glass again. His eyes glinted wickedly in the moonlight. 'Rebecca,' he said softly, 'will take good care of you while you are here. And she likes whisky, too.'

The girl was suddenly by my side. Her teeth gleamed the whitest of white as she smiled down at me. At close quarters, I was aware of a dark and sinuous beauty about her that looked much more likely to be Hausa in its origin than that of the squat swamp dwellers who inhabited these humid southern lands.

The night air pulsated. The drumbeat had become louder, more insistent, throbbing out its sensual invitation through the dark veil of Africa towards us. I felt a tiny nudge at my shoulder and I looked round. The girl was holding out a glass which she had brought through from the kitchen. I sighed resignedly and removed the bottle from Pisspot's clasp. Her eyes were huge and steady upon mine and they glowed like the eyes of a cat in the half-light as I poured her a drink.

She pulled up a chair and sat down between us. I put the cork firmly back in the bottle. 'Pisspot,' I said, 'drink up and let's eat. Then we'll walk down to the village. We have much dancing to do tonight, you and me and Rebecca.'

The girl got up and went through to the kitchen to fetch some plates. I watched the graceful sway of her body as she disappeared into the gloom. Definitely Hausa, I thought. And definitely far too good-looking to be Pisspot's daughter.

What with one thing and another, it looked like being a long and busy night.